NON-INVASIVE

DATA

GOVERNANCE

The Path of Least Resistance and Greatest Success

first edition

Robert S. Seiner

Published by:
Technics Publications, LLC
2 Lindsley Road
Basking Ridge, NJ 07920 USA

http://www.TechnicsPub.com

Cover design by Mark Brye

Copyright © 2014 by Robert S. Seiner

ISBN, print ed.   9781935504856
ISBN, Kindle ed.   9781935504863
ISBN, ePub ed.   9781935504870

First Printing 2014

Library of Congress Control Number: 2014947014

Table of Contents

Acknowledgements

It has taken me a long time to write this book. Not long in the length of time for the process, but rather for the elapsed time since I first formulated the words in my cranium. Over the years, many people have encouraged me to write a book or books, and I've always felt that my publication, *The Data Administration Newsletter* (TDAN.com), has given me enough opportunity to voice my opinions and thoughts about how to approach the issues of Data Administration, Data Management, Metadata Management, Knowledge Management, Data Stewardship, Data Governance, and specifically Non-Invasive Data Governance.

I have many people to thank for, well, everything. First of all, I would like to thank my wife, Cheryl, for supporting me in all my ventures or adventures over the years leading to this day. I also want to thank my daughters, Erin and Mandy, who have grown to be nice people, good people, sometimes difficult people. Hmm, I wonder where they got that from?

Both my wife and daughters seem to understand when I lock myself in my office for hours on end to do what I do, even though they're not certain they really know what I do. They do know that I do "PowerPoint for a living" (stolen from John Ladley many years ago). They know it has something to do with "managing data." They know I travel to the ends of the earth (okay, not really) to help organizations manage their data and information better. That's about it.

I want to thank my parents. May they rest in peace knowing that they raised me in such a way that I see them in practically everything I do and say. My father always taught me to be prepared and be strong. My mother taught me to be tough but loving at the same time. I think that summarizes the way I am quite well.

I want to thank my brothers, Henry and David, my sister, Harriet Ann, and their families for always being there to support me and each other as we have been through many wonderful times of celebration as well as our share of crises. I couldn't have asked for a better family, including everybody in the paragraphs above, and I wanted to publically thank you here.

I owe a debt of thanks to several key people who have helped me along the way through their good advice, opportunity to get exposure, being a good friend or helping to move the data governance industry forward. These people are, in no order of importance, Craig Mullins, Tony Shaw and all of the fantastic people at DATAVERSITY, Jean Schauer formerly at the BeyeNETWORK, Davida Berger, Gwen Thomas, and Joe Maggi. This list of friends and colleagues is always a list in progress. I hope and expect that you know who you are.

I want to thank my clients for putting their trust in me and the readers of my publications and attendees of my presentations and webinars for their attention, inspiration and kind words over the years.

I want to thank the authors who have contributed to The *Data Administration Newsletter* (TDAN.com) over the years. They are too many to name individually. I'll name a few who would not be mentioned otherwise—: Mike Gorman, Dave Hay, Barb von Halle, John Zachman, Ron Ross, Joe Celko, Daragh O'Brien, and Larry Burns. I think you know who you are, and I thank you for providing the TDAN.com readers with tremendous information, advice and experience over the years. My appreciation also goes out to the subscribers and readers of TDAN.com for being the whole reason for the publication in the first place.

I especially want to thank Hank Walshak for his help in compiling, editing, adding in, throwing out and rewording (so that the words made sense), as well as his overall project management of getting this book out the door. And Joyce Kane for her guidance and good-natured bantering. And of course, I thank Steve Hoberman, my publisher, for his encouragement and reinforcement in putting this book together and getting me off my bottom to complete this book.

And last of all, if you've purchased this book, thank you for bringing this work of art into your life. It's my fond hope that you will find many things in your journey through these pages that you find beneficial as you pursue building and implementing a successful Non-Invasive Data Governance™ program.

Chapter 1
Why This Book?

Many organizations attempt to gain support for formal data governance activities by expressing the value data governance can bring to their organizations. Although this is important—and needs to be different for each organization—other, related considerations come into play relative to data governance.

For example, consider what your organization cannot do because the data in your systems, databases, and resources, accumulated over the years, aren't governed to address what you cannot do. This question—what cannot your organization do?—isn't easy to ask, and the answers you receive may surprise you.

Consider some answers you can expect: We cannot compare costs across regions. We cannot track students' progress and see where they may be at risk. We cannot maximize the position of products in the store. We cannot match the records for an individual across their touch points to our organization. We cannot apply resources in the most cost-effective way. We cannot maximize our decision-making capabilities based on the data we have.

All of these *cannot* responses hinder how an organization grows and prospers. The data are at the core of addressing these concerns. And governing the data with a formal non-invasive approach that's shaped to the culture of an organization may be something to consider. I have been focusing on the Non-Invasive Data Governance™ approach for many years. That's what this book is about.

This book presents a totally new approach to selling data governance to your organization so that higher management can give the green light to proceed with the definition, delivery and administration of such a program. I've written about putting the necessary components of data governance into place so that you can deliver successful and sustainable data governance in your organization.

Two questions typically asked by people selling the need for data governance in their organizations are:

> 1. *What will it take to convince our management to apply resources, time, and money to building and operating a data governance program?*
>
> 2. *How do we get management to understand the importance of data governance?*

There are no simple answers to these questions. And this book is not targeted at trying to specifically answer these questions for your organization. Every organization, in its own way, prioritizes how it spends resources, time, and money. Each organization has a way to determine if data governance is important and valuable enough to pursue. And every organization has its way of making decisions about what will and will not be done.

Instead, I offer these words of wisdom through this book to achieve the goals you have set for data governance in your organization with the hope that you consider the non-invasive approach as an option. A core set of messages for management around Non-Invasive Data Governance™ are provided in the next section. But let's start with defining "data governance."

DEFINITION OF DATA GOVERNANCE

I define data governance this way:

> *Data governance is the formal execution and enforcement of authority over the management of data and data-related assets.*

The truth is that some organizations I've worked with have tamed this definition so that it isn't as scary sounding, or harsh, or in your face. They have developed definitions more in line with my definition of Non-Invasive Data Governance. For example:

> *Formalizing behavior around the definition, production, and usage of data to manage risk and improve quality and usability of selected data.*

Formalizing and guiding behavior over the definition, production, and use of information and information-related assets.

Notice that both definitions begin with "formalizing behavior." Formalizing behavior and holding people accountable are the two basic tenets of the Non-Invasive Data Governance approach. Formalizing behavior assumes that a sense of data governance is already taking place.

To stay non-invasive, organizations should:

- Identify people who informally already have a level of accountability for the data they define, produce and use to complete their jobs or functions. To do this, an organization must first design a data governance operating model of roles and responsibilities that aligns with the way the organization operates today. A successful operating model doesn't require you to fit your organizational components into its model. A successful operating model allows you to overlay its framework over existing, organizational components. You'll find detailed information about creating an operating model of roles and responsibilities in Chapter 6.

- Identify and govern existing escalation paths and decision-making capabilities from a perspective that's positive—how and why they are working—and negative—why they don't always work—and then leverage what's working while addressing opportunities to improve.

- Recognize people for what they do with data and help them formalize their behaviors so that they benefit others potentially impacted by their behaviors. Often, decisions are made in the heat of battle or in daily operations that result in positive and negative consequences for other people along the data lifecycle of definition, production, use, and reframing.

By including the term, "governance," data governance requires the administration of something. In this case, data governance refers to administering, or formalizing, discipline (behavior) around the management of data. Rather than making the discipline appear threatening and difficult, my suggestion is to follow a Non-Invasive Data Governance approach that focuses on formalizing what already exists and addressing opportunities for improvement.

MESSAGES FOR MANAGEMENT

The first reaction to the term "data governance" is often one of disdain or fear. The term "governance," like "government," conveys the impression that a program focusing on governance will include a number of laws or rules about the relationships people have with data. When speaking about relationships with data, these relationships simply define, produce, and use data as part of one's regular job. Thus, if people expect that we'll add laws governing their relationship to data, the first reaction will likely be fright or wariness relative to the value that data governance will add. People may even conclude that data governance will interfere with their responsibilities.

I'd like to offer you two sets of messages to use when sharing your approach to data governance in the hopes of getting people to ask you *how* your organization can achieve data governance—and, specifically, a Non-Invasive Data Governance approach—rather than *why* data governance is necessary.

CALMING MANAGEMENT'S NERVES ABOUT DATA MANAGEMENT

If you follow the Non-Invasive Data Governance approach, or are interested in following this approach, these five messages are critical for management:

1. **We are already governing data, but we are doing it informally.** People in the organization already have responsibility for data. You should inventory who does what with data and provide an operating model of roles and responsibilities that best suits your organization. At some level, you will need someone with an enterprise view and responsibility for data that cuts across the silos in your organization and manage data as a shared resource. This will be our biggest yet doable challenge, because we don't naturally manage data as a shared and enterprise-wide resource.

2. **We can formalize how we govern data by putting structure around what we are doing now.** People in your organization work in

operational, tactical, strategic, and support roles around data. We need to know who they are and put formal structure around who is responsible, accountable, consulted, and informed about the business rules and regulations associated with the data they define, produce, and use.

3. **We can improve our data governance.** Our data governance efforts can help us improve how we *manage risks* associated with compliance, classification, security, and business rules affecting our data. People in our organization potentially put us at risk every day when they're not assured of knowing the rules associated with their handling of data. Our efforts to *improve the quality* of data must be *coordinated and cooperative* across business units using the formal structure mentioned above. Quality assurance requires that operational and tactical staff have the ability to record, track, and resolve known data quality issues. Our organization can immediately improve how we *communicate* about data by recording and sharing information about who does what with data.

4. **We do not have to spend a lot of money on data governance.** Data governance does not have to be a costly endeavor. Depending on the approach we take, data governance may only cost the time we put into it. Data governance will require that one or more individuals spend the time defining and administering the program, but a large misconception is that data governance must be over and above the existing work efforts of an organization. We should avoid calling things "data governance processes" because this gives people the impression that formal behavior around data definition, production, and usage of data is the fault of data governance rather than the glue that ensures these behaviors are handled properly.

5. **We need structure. We should consider the Non-Invasive Data Governance approach.** We must follow a proven approach to data governance that does not threaten the people of our organization who participate in the program. Data governance will require that the business and the technology areas of the organization take formal and shared accountability for how data is governed. The participants in the

data governance program already have day jobs. We must add value and not interfere with what they do in their jobs. The goal of non-invasive data governance is to be transparent, supportive, and collaborative. These concepts lie at the heart of the implementation of the Non-Invasive Data Governance approach.

The first four messages above help to ease management's nerves and to help them realize that a variety of ways exist to communicate data governance within your organization. In this regard, it's important to remember that in most situations, people in your workplace will believe what you tell them, provided your message educates them and offers a positive and fresh perspective on data governance.

Besides focusing on management, this second set of messages clarifies the heart of the Non-Invasive Data Governance approach by emphasizing the truly non-invasive nature of the approach. Let me introduce these messages by relating a simple story about a recent presentation I delivered.

At the beginning of this presentation to data enthusiasts from dozens of companies and organizations, I asked attendees to raise their hands if their organizations were doing data governance. About half of the audience members' hands went up.

To make an important point, I posed the same question again by saying, "Okay, this time, I want everybody to raise a hand when I ask the same question." I asked the same question and everybody's hand went up. To everyone's surprise, I said, "Now that's more like it." I received some confused glances, but by the end of the session, the attendees understood this important message:

> *All organizations already govern data. They may do*
> *it informally, sometimes inefficiently, often*
> *ineffectively, but they already govern data. And they*
> *all can do it better.*

Let's use a data warehousing or master data management environment as an example because you likely have one or more of these, have been involved in building one of them, or at least have heard of them if you're reading this book.

When you were building your data warehouse, one or more individuals had the responsibility of *defining* what data went in the data warehouse. Some of these individuals had the responsibility to *produce* data through one or multiple extracts, transform, and loading processes. Other individuals had the responsibility for *using* the warehouse data for its intended purpose. For each of the systems or data resources that fed the data warehouse, someone was responsible for defining, producing, and using that data. Responsibilities abounded throughout your data warehousing environment.

Decisions were, and still are, reached around your data warehouse; issues were solved, security was applied, metadata were made available, and data were exported for individual use. All these occurrences happened around data warehousing and business intelligence.

You may do some of these activities well. Other activities may need to be improved. These occurrences represent a microcosm of the rest of your enterprise's existing data governance. Somewhere, somehow, the governance of data is going on. But often, no formal thing called "data governance" exists. But to a large degree, you are "executing and enforcing authority over the management of data and data-related resources," according to my definition of data governance.

Wouldn't it be great if we could put some structure around how we already govern our data without throwing a lot of money and resources at the problem? The truth is you can. This book is all about how to do it by implementing data governance in a non-invasive way, taking advantage of the levels of governance that already exist in your organization, and addressing opportunities to improve.

At first glance, implementing a data governance program may appear to be a huge challenge. This may be partly true because data governance presents challenges. The challenges will become apparent because of the organization's size and the complexities of its business, but not because of data governance per se.

WHAT TO TELL MANAGEMENT

This next set of messages focuses on getting past some of the major misperceptions people in organizations have when they consider data governance.

1. **Avoid selling data governance as a huge challenge.** And if your management already thinks that data governance will be a major challenge, try to calm them by referring to the Messages for Management in this chapter. Data governance can be implemented in a non-threatening, non-interfering, non-culture-changing, non-invasive way that will reduce the challenges people in your company may have. Data governance need not be implemented all at once. In fact, most organizations that successfully introduce data governance implement their programs incrementally. This includes the scope of data that's governed domain-wise and organizationally as well as the level of governance of formal behavior applied to the data.

2. **Emphasize that data governance is not a technical solution.** A technical component to your data governance program will likely exist. But there might not be one. The fact is you can't purchase software or hardware that will be your data governance solution. What's more, simple tools can be developed internally to help organizations govern peoples' behaviors relative to data.

3. **Emphasize that people's behaviors, not data, are governed.** Data governance formalizes the behavior of people for the definition, production, and usage of data. The emphasis is on formalizing peoples' behaviors, not the behavior of data. Data behaves the way people behave. Technology may help you govern the behaviors of people, but data does what you tell it to. Because peoples' behaviors are governed, many organizations consider data governance to be a process-driven discipline. That is partially true. Getting people to do the right thing at the right time is a large part of governance. But organizations that sell data governance as an entirely new governance process struggle because of the perceived invasiveness of this approach. Governance should first formalize behavior around existing processes and only add to people's workloads as a last resort.

4. **Emphasize that data governance is an evolution, not a revolution.** As mentioned earlier, data governance won't be completed all at once. Different organizations transition themselves into a data governance state in different ways. Some organizations focus early on specific domains or subject areas of data. Other organizations concentrate on specific business areas, divisions, units, or applications rather than implementing all across the organization at once. Still other organizations focus on a combination of two or three specific domains within business units using specific applications. No single correct way exists for data governance to evolve in your company. Nonetheless, I can assure you that employees will resist if you treat it as a revolution.

Key Points

- Data governance is the formal execution and enforcement of authority over the management of data and data related assets.

- We are already governing data; we are doing it informally. We can formalize how we govern data by putting structure around what we're presently doing.

- We can improve how we manage data risk and secure data, data quality, and quality assurance without spending a lot of money.

- We do not have to spend a lot of money.

- Avoid selling data governance as a huge challenge.

- Emphasize that data governance is not a technical solution.

- Stress that peoples' behaviors, not data, are governed.

- Focus on data governance as an evolution, not revolution.

I started focusing on a Non-Invasive Data Governance perspective many years before I started using this term to describe my approach. When I worked in the corporate world, my first data governance effort focused on data stewards, which will be discussed in Chapter 7. The approach to stewards centered on helping the people of the organization do their jobs without giving them the impression that they were being given any responsibility beyond what they already had. At first, it was clear that my approach to data governance would be non-invasive.

Now, after implementing data governance and information governance programs in this fashion for many years, I can honestly say that my approach has become less invasive over time. Think about it. Your data governance program can be either non-invasive—less intrusive, less threatening, less expensive, but more effective—or invasive—about command and control. I call the invasive approach the two-by-four approach. You decide. But read on before you do.

I'm often asked, "How can you possibly implement a data governance program in a non-invasive way?" The organizations that follow the approach described in this book tell me that the term "Non-Invasive Data Governance" is what attracted them to this approach.

The term aims directly at the heart of the concerns many organizations have about data governance in the first place. In general they are as follows:

- Most organizations view data governance as something over and above normal work efforts that threatens the existing work culture of an organization. I emphasize that *it does not have to be this way*.

- Most organizations have a difficult time getting people to adopt data governance best practices because of a common belief that data governance is about command and control. *It does not have to be this way, either.*

- I firmly state that data governance is the execution and enforcement of authority over the management of data. But nowhere in this definition does it say that data governance has to be invasive or threatening to the work, people, and culture of an organization.

Non-Invasive Data Governance can be summed up in a few brief statements. With the Non-Invasive Data Governance approach:

- The responsibilities of data stewards are identified and recognized, formalized, and engaged according to their existing responsibilities rather than making them feel as though you're assigning them more work.

- The governance of data is applied to existing policies, operating procedures, practices, and methodologies rather than starting by introducing or emphasizing new processes or methods.

- The governance of data augments and supports all data integration, risk management, business intelligence, and master data management activities consistently across an enterprise rather than imposing inconsistent rigor to these initiatives.

- Specific attention is paid to assuring senior management's understanding of a practical and non-threatening, yet effective, approach to governing data that will be taken to mediate ownership and promote stewarding of data as a cross-organization asset rather than maintaining governance in silo fashion or as something one is told to do.

- Best practices and key concepts of the non-threatening approach to data governance are communicated effectively and are compared to existing practices to identify and leverage strengths and enable the ability to address opportunities to improve.

DATA GOVERNANCE IS NOT A PROCESS

I have a pet peeve when it comes to talking about data governance. This pet peeve is directed at getting people to understand that data governance, in itself, is not a process. It strikes me as unproductive when people talk about the "process or processes of data governance." With the non-invasive approach to data governance, the governance and formality are applied to processes that already exist.

I dislike this term "process" because I believe that calling processes "data governance processes" causes more damage than good. The intent of being non-invasive with your approach to data governance is to be transparent to the organization by applying governance to existing processes rather than leading the organization to think that all of the processes that are governed were caused by the activities of data governance. If you are non-invasive in your approach, you recognize that these processes existed, or were created for a purpose, before any talk about data governance and that the program is focusing on getting the right individuals involved in the process at the right time and for the right reason.

I usually refer to this application of data governance as the "Data Governance Bill of Rights." But before I detail how the Bill of Rights lies at the core of a Non-Invasive Data Governance approach, allow me to share with you a quick anecdote about jumpstarting a Non-Invasive Data Governance program even in the toughest of financial circumstances.

DATA GOVERNANCE AND DANCING IN THE RAIN

Every once in a while, when my younger daughter, Mandy, was young, she'd come to me with a quote she read somewhere and she'd want me to consider using it as the weekly quote on the front pages of *The Data Administration Newsletter* (TDAN.com).

Once, when Mandy was 12 years old, she approached me with this quote: "Life isn't about waiting for the storm to pass. It's about learning to dance in the rain."

I immediately thought, "How can this quote relate to data governance and specifically my reader base?" I saw an instant connection. I quickly asked, "Who said that?" Mandy's pushing-teen-dom response was, "Somebody."

I had heard this quote at least once before, and after a quick Internet search, I found the quote in many places. I found that the quote is not attributed to anybody in particular. I typically do not use un-acknowledged quotes in my writings, but the more I thought about the quote, the more I thought it would be great to apply it to data governance.

THE MIDDLE OF A STORM

Chances are you're feeling the storm if you work in corporate America (or in corporate anywhere), if you work in the private sector or public sector or in education, or even if you're self-employed. Financial times are difficult for everybody. The stock market takes dives and recovers, but it still remains volatile. Hence the retirement of the word "retirement" from many people's vocabularies. Unemployment is at high levels. Companies are cutting back. Projects are delayed if not canceled. Coworkers of many years are being shown the door. Companies are becoming leaner, if not meaner, in the way they are downsizing. The storm is here. It's hanging right above us, and we're all feeling it.

Information Technology (IT) isn't the only part of these organizations under dark clouds. Business areas are feeling the pinch as well. In fact, belt tightening and withheld funding impacts everybody in an organization. Data governance programs that impact both IT and business areas have become the latest victims of lack of funding in many organizations.

These organizations recognize that data governance is important when it comes to compliance, regulatory control, classification, security, privacy, and the overall management of data-oriented risk. Nonetheless, the storm has caused many of these organizations to hang an awning over data governance and wait for the storm to pass.

Most organizations understand the need for data governance. And most individuals will raise their hands when asked if they have significant room for improvement in governing data. If you're uncertain where your organization stands, I suggest that you review The Data Governance Test in Chapter 4 and perform a self-evaluation of where your organization stands on data governance in comparison to where it wants to be.

I'd be surprised if you come to the conclusion that the storm isn't having some impact on your data governance program.

LIFE ISN'T ABOUT WAITING FOR THE STORM TO PASS

Certainly, one option is to wait for the storm to pass. Gather under the awning. If you know how long the storm will last, please share this with my readers and me. Experts say that we're seeing signs that the poor economy has reached its bottom. Yet even optimistic experts say that it may be a long while, if ever, before the economy comes back anywhere close to where it had been. The days of excess may be behind us. The days of overstaffing, over-budgeting, and consultant-laden organizations may also be things of the past. The days of heavy financial scrutiny are here, and all indications are that they will not leave anytime soon. So grab your raincoat, galoshes, umbrella, and rubber duckies, because the storm may be with us a while.

It may be storming outside (and sometimes inside) your organization's walls, but the problems and opportunities that surround the management of data are here to stay. Chances are your management still considers managing the risk around data—including compliance, security, privacy, classification, and protection—to be important. The odds are that management may also continue to look for ways to improve the value they get from their data through business intelligence, master data management, and package implementations. These are the types of initiatives, however, that may be relegated to the back burner.

Here's a simple suggestion worth considering: Do what you can now to address these problems. More importantly, find ways to capitalize on opportunities at hand, even if little or no funding is available.

IT'S ABOUT LEARNING TO DANCE IN THE RAIN

Here's something you probably haven't thought about the definition of "dancing." Dancing is defined as moving rhythmically, usually to music, using prescribed or improvised steps and gestures [thefreedictionary.com].

Last time I checked, dancing didn't cost any money at all. Dancing in the rain doesn't cost much either (and you probably have more room). Wait. That's all wrong. Mandy—remember her as the one who came up with this sappy quote to begin with—dances all the time. Most of the time it's free when she is constantly fluttering—sorry, moving rhythmically around the house to music in her head—but the dance lessons and theatre arts training are costing something. OK, so dancing is not always free.

Data governance programs are not always free either. With proper management, however, a data governance program, particularly a Non-Invasive Data Governance program, can provide value to the organization the likes of which it has never seen before and at an extremely low cost. Let me emphasize that again: **A data governance program can provide a high level of value to an organization without spending heaps of money.**

What can we do to move our organization forward while it rains like the dickens? What can we do to get the focus where it needs to be to put a data governance program in place? Perhaps we can step outside into the storm for a moment and look for things that we as an organization can do right now to put the basic components of a Non-Invasive Data Governance program in place without really feeling the impact of the storm. Hey! I call that dancing. And who cares if you get a little wet?

Here are a few things that you can do right now to step outside in the storm, dance a little bit, and build the solid foundation for a Non-Invasive Data Governance program:

1. Convince your management that, depending on the approach you take, a data governance program only costs the time you put into it. You will need to explain that the primary cost of a Non-Invasive Data Governance program is the availability of human resources to manage the program. Incremental costs only come through expansion and acceptance and formalized involvement.

2. Identify a person who will have the responsibility for defining what data governance will mean for the organization. This individual should have access to business and IT areas, resources charged with improving

value, quality, and process through improved data-risk management, data integration, and data governance.

3. Select a project or an activity to work with, to learn from, and to assign the appropriate people to define, produce, and use specific data related to the activity. In other words, learn from your present state of information security, business intelligence, master-data management, scorecards, and dashboards. You already have some level of governance in place. Learn from it.

4. Record information about the people engaged in data activities related to this project in a structured manner.

5. While Numbers 3 and 4 take place, have the person from Number 2 work with his or her colleagues to define a practical data governance framework of roles and responsibilities. These roles and responsibilities should address operational, tactical, strategic, executive, and support management and map the roles of the framework to the existing level of governance around the data for each partnering initiative.

6. Pardon this bold hint: Seek mentoring assistance from someone who has your best interests in mind and who has implemented effective Non-Invasive Data Governance programs in the past. Use this mentor to provide knowledge transfer and to pinpoint resourcing—assessment, action plan, policy, awareness, communication—as needed throughout the program development.

CASE STUDY: DANCING IN THE RAIN

Several years ago, I had the privilege of working alongside a gentleman who had been given the responsibility to put a data governance program in place for his company, but who had also been given no resources to work with or budget to speak of related to data governance. Does this story sound familiar to you?

This gentleman, let's call him the Data Governance Lead, had no managerial tenure or ambitions. Yet he felt strongly that managing data as a valuable corporate asset was the right thing for his company to do and the right thing to help him focus his career on something meaningful and assertive.

The Data Governance Lead recognized he had an uphill battle to fight. He recognized that the budget cycle was something difficult to break into. He found that people in his organization were used to performing their jobs in a habitually comfortable way and that they had no interest in applying or having formal discipline applied to the way they defined, produced, and used data. He found that people were entirely focused on their own jobs and performing well. They didn't care about the impact they had on how the company operated or whether they adversely impacted the bottom line. He recognized that people were more concerned about keeping their jobs than anything else.

The Data Governance Lead recognized he had a problem and would have to dance a little or a lot to get his data governance program off the ground. And he was right.

The Data Governance Lead decided he could work on several things in a sort of stealth pattern to move his organization in the right direction of data governance. Here's what he did while he danced in the rain:

1. The Data Governance Lead decided to document what he called "governance metadata" about the domains, or subject areas, of data that he thought were most valuable to the organization. This governance metadata included things like what valuable data existed in what systems and databases, and who in the organization defined, produced and, used these data.

2. He documented the steps that particular data took to make their way into the key performance indicators (KPIs) for the company.

3. The Data Governance Lead documented how the definitions and uses of data differed depending on the people he spoke with or the systems and databases containing the data.

4. He identified and recorded the people who felt they had (or who were recognized as having) decision-making responsibility around the data.

5. The Data Governance Lead identified and recorded information about what the company couldn't do because of the present state of the data that fed the KPIs.

6. He took many other steps to detail the information he was going to need to help people to understand how the lack of formal data governance around the data was costing the company money and prevented the company from getting the most value out of its data or making the best possible decisions.

7. While the Data Governance Lead was carrying out steps 1 to 6, he was separately discovering ways that data governance would enable the company to resolve specific issues pertaining to the KPI data.

8. He effectively addressed something extremely meaningful to the higher managers while he detailed the business case for implementing a formal data governance program with resources and time allocated to the effort.

In fact, the steps the Data Governance Lead took were non-invasive. He didn't interfere with any of the other activities in the organization or didn't give anybody additional work over and above their existing responsibilities as he gathered his information in a non-invasive way to make the case for data governance.

As a matter of course, and through convincing his direct management, the Data Governance Lead was able to meet the chief operating officer of the company for a short time to share and explain his findings and the case for data governance.

In effect, the Data Governance Lead danced in the rain until the sun shone down upon him.

DON'T BE AFRAID TO GET WET

Mandy, and a few people before her, said that "Life isn't about waiting for the storm to pass. It's about learning to dance in the rain." Well, it's still raining pretty hard in a lot of places. Your first option is to sit around waiting for the rain to stop. And we all know that could take a long time. Waiting for the storm to pass may or may not lead to you still being there when the clouds disappear and the sun comes out once more. Your second option is to get outside and dance in the rain. Find things that you can do on the rainy days with a restrained budget and with lack of resources. Find ways that you can build a data governance program now, even when your organization doesn't consciously apply significant resources to putting the program in place.

I assure you there are things that you can be doing right now, for little or no cost, like dancing in the rain to open management's eyes to how effective the Non-Invasive Data Governance approach can be. Take that step forward and start building and demonstrating cost-effective results from your own non-invasive approach.

As Gene Kelly, from my hometown of Pittsburgh, Pennsylvania, once sang and danced in the rain, "What a glorious feeling, I'm happy again."

Key Points

- Although data governance is "the execution and enforcement of authority over the management of data," nowhere in this definition does it say that data governance has to be invasive or threatening to the work, people, and culture of an organization.

- Data steward responsibilities are identified, recognized, formalized, and engaged according to their existing responsibility rather than being assigned or handed to people as more work.

- The governance of data is applied to existing policies, standard operating procedures, practices, and methodologies rather than being introduced or emphasized as new processes or methods.

Chapter 3
Business Value of Data Governance

Data governance means different things to different people and organizations. Several definitions are floating around the industry. The niche data governance consultants have theirs, the large system integrators have theirs, and the large global consultancies have theirs.

They all define the same thing just in different ways. Sometimes organizations use the terms "data governance" and "data stewardship" interchangeably. At other times, they use the term, "non-invasive" to describe the approach they take to data governance.

I have my definition and have shared this with you earlier in the first chapter of this book, but let me repeat it here. Please let me explain.

The most important question that begs for an answer about data governance is this:

What does it mean to govern data?

Please take a moment to think about and answer this question. We all know that data governance is necessary, but what does it mean to have your data governed?

The best place to start is to define the term "govern" as it relates to data. To do this, I have taken the FreeDictionary.com definition of "govern" and wrapped the words "to" and "data" around each identifying characteristic—the part of the definition that tells you how that term differs from other terms. This wrapper around the identifying characteristics of the word "govern" makes the definition easier to read, and doing so puts it in the context of data management.

I have taken each of these identifying characteristics of what it means to govern something and placed them in the table below with a description of what governing data means in relationship to the characteristic.

	ing Characteristics of Governing
blic policy and affairs of data	**Governing data means** that data policy takes the form of written and approved (this is a key point) corporate or organizational documents.
	Governing data means that you have a data governance policy. This policy may be hidden under the name of information security policy, privacy policy, or data classification policy (e.g. highly confidential, confidential, sensitive, public data, or something else).
	Governing data means that your organization leverages the effort invested in development and approval of the policy rather than allowing the policy to become shelf ware. As shelf ware, few people know how the policy is associated with the data they define, produce, and use daily.
To exercise the sovereign authority of data	**Governing data means** that a way exists to resolve a difference of opinion on a cross-business data issue.
	Governing data means that somebody or some group of individuals is the authority or has the authority to make decisions concerning the data.
	Governing data means that an escalation path exists from the operational to the tactical to the strategic levels of the organization for decision-making. Rarely does governing data require escalation of data issues to the executive level.
To control the speed or magnitude of data	**Governing data means** that data are shared according to the classification (confidential, sensitive, public) rules associated with that data.
	Governing data means that the creation of new versions of the same data is scrutinized closely to manage and eliminate data redundancy.
	Governing data means that people don't place critical or confidential data in harm's way by quickly, and without knowing the rules, making copies of data that fails to follow the same scrutiny and governance as data in native form.
To regulate data	**Governing data means** that appropriate processes are put in place and monitored to manage the definition, production, and usage of data at all levels of an organization.
	Governing data means that proactive and reactive processes are defined, approved, and followed at all levels of the organization. Situations where these procedures aren't followed can be identified, prevented, and resolved.
	Governing data means that the appropriate behaviors around data are brought to the forefront of your staff members thought processes rather than being pushed to the back of their minds as an "inconvenience" or a "nice to have."
To control the actions or behaviors of data	**Governing data means** that appropriate processes are put in place and monitored to manage the definition, production, and usage of data at all levels of the organization.
	Governing data means that proactive and reactive processes are defined,

	approved, and followed at all levels of the organization and that situations where these procedures aren't followed can be identified, prevented, and resolved.
	Governing data means that the appropriate behaviors around data are brought to the forefront of your staff's thought processes rather than being pushed to the back of their minds as an "inconvenience" or a "nice to have."
To keep under control and to restrain data	**Governing data means** that access to data is managed, secured, and auditable by classification (confidential, sensitive, public) and that processes and responsibilities are put in place to assure that access privileges are granted only to appropriate individuals.
	Governing data means that all individuals understand the rules associated with importing data into spreadsheets, loading data to laptops, transmitting data, or any other activity that removes data from the native source.
	Governing data means that the rules associated with managing hardcopy versions of data are well documented and communicated to individuals who generate, receive, or distribute these hard copies.
To exercise a deciding or determining influence of data	**Governing data means** that the right people are involved at the right time for the right reasons to assure that the right decisions are made about the right data.
	Governing data means that the information about who in the organization does what with the data is completely recorded, shared, and understood across the organization. This provides the ability to get the rights right.
	Governing data means that a formal escalation path exists for known data issues that moves from operational (business unit specific) to the tactical (cross-business unit) to the strategic (enterprise) and to the persons identified as the authorities on that specific use of the data.
To exercise political authority over data	**Governing data means** that somebody or some group of people have the authority to make decisions for the enterprise about data that impacts the enterprise.
	Governing data means that the political nature of decision-making is leveraged in making the tactical and strategic decisions that best benefit the enterprise.
	Governing data means a formal escalation path exists for known data issues that move from operational (business unit specific) to the tactical (cross business unit) to the strategic (enterprise) and to persons identified as the authorities on that specific use of that data.

The statements I've listed with each of the identifying characteristics of the definition of the word "govern" should help you get a jump-start explaining what it means to govern data. Once you have answered the question of what it means to govern data, the next question you may hear is:

What's the best way to govern data?

And to that question you can answer, "The Non-Invasive Data Governance approach."

I started this book by saying that many organizations attempt to gain support for formal data governance activities by describing the value data governance adds to their organizations. As you'll see in this chapter, expressing this value of data governance is important for many organizations to get the go-ahead to begin putting a program in place.

I suggest that you consider what your organization *cannot do* because the data in your systems, databases, and resources that have accumulated over the years do not allow you to do it. I provided examples of what organizations can't do in Chapter 1.

The combination of the value you articulate to your business sponsors and the list of things your business folks cannot do becomes a powerful one-two punch of information to share with your potential business sponsor(s).

WHO DEFINES THE VALUE?

Two primary groups of people will define how data governance will add value at your organization:

- First, those who have the responsibility for defining and deploying your data governance program.

- Second, everybody else.

The data governance team (which we'll cover in Chapter 10), or those individuals who want to form a data governance team, typically take on the responsibility to persuade management that data governance is important and that time, resources, and effort should be spent on putting a data governance program in place. These individuals may not be a formal team at the beginning, but they have an idea for governance and spend significant energy selling the virtues of data governance. This is a common occurrence.

I'm not suggesting that we change how the data governance team operates when it comes to selling the program. I do recommend that this team partner with people in the business areas to define the value of data governance for the organization. The team needs to prompt the business areas to speak up about where they believe data governance will add value for them.

To get the business areas to speak up this way, I recommend that you take these steps:

1. Educate people in the business areas on what data governance is and the approach you're taking as an organization to achieve the goal.

2. Ask specific questions to prompt them to speak up about things they cannot do and the issues that they live with day to day concerning the data they define, produce, and use.

3. Document people you've spoken to and what they said. This demonstrates that the value is defined by the businesses rather than by the data governance team.

This sounds pretty easy on paper, but let's walk through each of these steps quickly.

EDUCATE THE BUSINESS ON YOUR DATA GOVERNANCE APPROACH

This step requires that you define your approach ahead of time and that your approach is practical and doable in your organization. The approach will often include a best practice, an operating model of roles and responsibilities, an action plan and a communications plan at the least. The approach often includes an inventory of data and stewards and a mapped-out plan for how data governance will be applied through existing and new processes.

This is one place where the non-invasive approach to data governance adds the most value. Start with the Messages for Management in Chapter 1 to assure that data governance is not all about command and control and can be free of these restraints.

Data is a universal business problem. Many business areas will give you time to introduce them to the subject and your specific approach to data governance if they:

- Recognize a problem in the form of something they cannot do.

- Believe you will add value to what they do.

- Know you have their best interests in mind when you work with them.

LEARN WHAT THE BUSINESS CANNOT DO

When having conversations with people in the business areas, your mission should be to get to the root of how formalized discipline around data will add value to what they do. Therefore, let's start there:

- Ask them what they cannot do because of the lack of availability, the quality, or their knowledge about the data.

- Ask them where they get their data, how they spend their time working with data, and if there are things that could be made easier. These questions lay at the core of their pain.

- Ask the business areas to give you permission to use what they tell you in the next steps.

Getting the business areas to tell the data governance team the value of data governance takes a lot of the pressure off of the data governance team. If the team is viewed as working for the best interests of the business areas, this will free up some of the data governance team's time because the team will spend less time selling and more time building out their program.

DOCUMENT THE BUSINESS VALUE FROM THE BUSINESS

The last step is to document and use the information you get from the business areas. It works even better if you can get the business areas themselves to take the information to senior managers to persuade them that data governance is necessary. We all know this doesn't happen naturally. Typically, someone has to force the issue.

Keep a log of the individuals and business areas you reach out to. Document specifically how they answered the questions from the previous paragraphs and connect the people with what they said. If they gave you permission in the previous step, don't be afraid to quote them in your presentation of this information to management. Make it clear to management that executives can revisit what the business(es) said to support their business value.

Document the expected business value of what you heard using a formula that works for your organization or the business value statements shared in the next section.

CASE STUDY: PLANT MANAGER NEEDS DATA MANAGEMENT SOLUTION

Every once in a while, a business meeting occurs where a business person explodes with information that helps the person calling the meeting with his or her mission, whatever that mission may be. Let me share one example with you here.

A global manufacturing company was working on gaining support for its data governance program from a select number of plant managers. Some plant managers were in the United States, and several others were located at plants in Europe.

In the first business meeting with a plant manager, the data governance manager began the meeting by explaining data governance and the non-invasive approach. The plant manager absorbed everything the manager and I shared, and it seemed like a typical meeting where a lot of information was accepted quite well.

And then it happened. The plant manager told us that he appreciated that we had taken the time to put him on our schedule. The plant manager said that he had compiled a list of things he could not do because the data of the organization did not support what he wanted to do.

The plant manager shared that he, and therefore the company, could not identify the best place to manufacture certain products because of the cost of raw materials and the cost to transport these raw materials to the plant. He went on to explain that he could not compare costs across regions when it came to distributing product served by different plants in the vicinity. He had a list of business problems that all pertained to needing access to data to help reach key decisions like these.

At the time, I suggested to my client that we should use what the plant manager said to make the case for how data governance would add business value by addressing the issues the plant manager had raised. I also recommended using this information in meetings with the other plant managers to get them thinking the same way.

Getting the business to speak up and make the case for data governance decreases the need for the data governance team to make the case. Instead, the data governance team has the responsibility to get this information to the people making the decision. By letting the business make the case for data governance, no one can say that data governance is an IT project solely intended for IT gain. Data governance becomes a business solution.

BUSINESS-VALUE STATEMENT SAMPLES

When used in the business world, the term, value statement, can be defined as brief verbiage that demonstrates a cause-and-effect relationship between a business action and the business value that action gains. Anybody who has been a consultant or an employee (or anybody who has tried to convince someone to do something) has used a value statement to demonstrate the worthiness of some type of endeavor.

In the information technology (IT) areas of a business or organization, value statements help to convince senior management to use a new type of technology, to put money toward a new vendor package, and to eliminate redundant systems. Value statements are also used to develop or enhance a business intelligence or data warehousing initiative and for other situations that require some level of funding and that we all can relate to. Value statements have now become a major contributor to convincing senior managements of companies and organizations that they should pursue the design and deployment of data governance.

A Non-Invasive Data Governance value statement may be defined as a cause-and-effect relationship between formalizing existing levels of governance (and putting a non-threatening program in place to govern data) and the business value that will be gained by governing data in this manner.

VALUE-STATEMENT FORMULAS

Over the years I have used a set of value statements to demonstrate the value of Non-Invasive Data Governance programs to clients. The formula I use for Non-Invasive Data Governance value statements is brief and to the point:

$$\textit{Organizations that do (X)}$$
$$\textit{demonstrate[1] business value improvements through}$$
$$\textit{(Y).}$$

Where (X) represents clearly defined actions and (Y) reflects business improvements that result from the actions.

In keeping with the Non-Invasive Data Governance approach, I keep my formula for value statements short and sweet. I do this because the idea of a longer or more complex value statement offers the impression that there are many components to the value that comes from data governance, and that deriving value from a data governance program is more complex than it needs to be. I prefer to keep my value statements to two parts to reduce the appearance of complexity.

The point of this formula is to demonstrate that using an easy-to-use tool like a value statement, with a consistent formula for reading and understanding, articulates simply the value of a Non-Invasive Data Governance program to senior management or anybody in the organization who can influence change.

BUSINESS VALUE STATEMENTS FOR NON-INVASIVE DATA GOVERNANCE

Here is a list of Non-Invasive Data Governance business value statements I've used in recent presentations. The (X) component of my value statement formula is shown in **bold**, and the (Y) component of my formula is shown in *italics*.

---

[1] *Demonstrate* or some other verb.

- **Organizations that have senior managers and business unit Leaders who understand, support, and offer direction for a Non-Invasive Data Governance approach and programs** *assure themselves of less risk and better acceptance by general staff around the management of data for the short- and long-term success of the program.*

- **Organizations that identify, record, and make available information about the people who define, produce and use specific core and corporate critical data** *demonstrate efficient and effective coordination, cooperation, and communications around these data.*

- **Organizations that document information about highly valued core and corporate critical data elements** *demonstrate improved understanding and business use of these data.*

- **Organizations that improve their ability to share information about data** *demonstrate better ability to respond to changes in regulatory and audit requirements.*

- **Organizations that make certain that the appropriate people are involved in specific tasks related to data management** *demonstrate the ability to eliminate replication and misuse of data, and improve their ability to integrate data based on corporate critical data element standards.*

- **Organizations that define and follow set processes and standard operating procedures for governing data—including requesting, sharing, defining, producing, and using data—** *demonstrate the ability to ensure that data will be shared according to data classification requirements (private, public, and sensitive data).*

- **Organizations that build and formalize data governance responsibilities into daily routine and methodology** *quickly view processes associated with data governance as non-threatening and habitual rather than over and above the existing work effort.*

- **Organizations that build, communicate effectively, and enforce stricter data management policies** *assure themselves of lower levels* *of enterprise risk when it comes to data management and data-compliance assessments.*

THE BOTTOM LINE

In the spirit of the value statements discussed in this chapter, I share with you a quick bottom-line conclusion to the use of value statements to demonstrate how a Non-Invasive Data Governance program will benefit your organization.

- **Organizations that are implementing Non-Invasive Data Governance programs** *typically look for return on investment and bottom-line impact from several areas: efficiency and effectiveness of data issue resolution, compliance and auditable demonstration, enterprise risk management, management, and employee decision-making empowerment rather than in dollars and cents.*

CASE STUDY: MANAGEMENT GIVES GO AHEAD FOR DATA GOVERNANCE PROGRAM

A telecommunications company engaged me to assist in implementing their data governance program in a non-invasive manner. This company had a problem communicating the value of data governance and the impact data governance would have on their ability to effectively retain and add new customers through the data they had about their customers.

This company wanted to show the cause and effect of data governance as an initial step in convincing senior management that a program was necessary. The use of a business value statement was the decided approach.

In a short time and through a facilitated session, the company was able to articulate clearly, using the formula described earlier in this chapter, several causes and effects of data governance specifically focused on their mission.

This company decided that if senior and business management understood data governance better and offered direction to the governance program, the program would have a better chance of success in the long run. Thus, they created a business value statement, similar to the first sample I shared, directed to their organization.

The company recognized the importance of metadata for the implementation of its data governance program and created business value statements similar to the second and third statement I just shared directed to their organization and their ability to record and share effective metadata.

The company adopted a data governance Bill of Rights (See Chapter 12) and got the right people involved in solving the right data issues, at the right time, using the right data. This led to the right solution for the problem or issue. The company developed business value statements incorporating the best ideas from the bulleted statements above directed at the impact these value statements would have on the business of retaining and adding new customers.

Key Points

- Data governance advocates in the organization must get the business people to speak up about the value they expect to receive from data governance.

- The two primary components of a business value to share with the business sponsors of data governance for your organization are 1) What business people can't do because the data don't support the activity, and 2) The business values that can be expected from putting formal data governance in place.

- The formula for building a business value statement is: Organizations that do (X, *demonstrate* business value improvements through (Y).

Chapter 4
Planning Your Data Governance Program

Several years ago, I worked with a client in the United States and Europe to develop a set of core principles associated with data governance. The principles we arrived at represent a finite and simplified view of what his organization set out to accomplish by deploying a formal data governance program.

Our intent and hope was that we would get the highest level of the client's organization to agree that these principles were important and that his company needed to accomplish what the principles stated. We also looked forward to senior management's signing a policy statement, the foundation for which was our principles.

I have used these principles in much of my consulting and in many of my presentations and webinars. That's because I think that the organizations I interact with should consider these principles as an easy way to describe the basics of data governance in the hope that senior management, however defined, will agree.

The graphic on the following page depicts how a data governance policy can break down into core principles that can be supported by dimensions of data quality. The graphic includes Tag Lines (quick phrased to help remember each principle) in bubbles attached to each principle. An explanation of each principle follows the graphic.

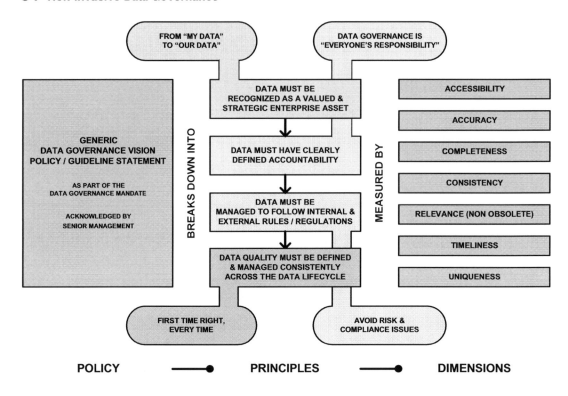

PRINCIPLE 1: RECOGNIZE DATA AS A VALUED AND STRATEGIC ENTERPRISE ASSET

From "My Data" to "Our Data"

RATIONALE

- Data comprise a valuable corporate resource. Accurate, timely data are the critical foundation for effective decision-making and customer service at a company.

IMPLICATIONS

- Carefully manage data to ensure they are clearly defined, properly accessed, and appropriately controlled. Company management and staff must be able to rely upon the accuracy of data and be able to obtain data when and where needed.

Data Governance Is "Everyone's Responsibility."

RATIONALE

- Most data have value for an organization beyond the uses of any one specific application. A company requires that data be shared and integrated at the enterprise level, consistent with information security and privacy policies.

- Data must be well defined to be sharable. And enterprise-shareable data must be defined consistently across the enterprise, with clear definitions available to all users.

- Wide access to data leads to efficiency and effectiveness in decision-making and provides timely response to information requests and service delivery.

IMPLICATIONS

- Shared data result in improved decisions. Maintaining a single source of timely, accurate data is less costly than maintaining several sources of data that aren't unique. Data are better aligned with cross-business requirements. Syntactic and semantic differences among databases will be minimized and applications will be more portable. Additionally, data management can change the data environment based on changing requirements or conditions with minimal impact to the applications.

- Data must be protected from unauthorized use and disclosure. Processes, procedures, and automated methods will be used to ensure the security of data.

- Access to data should be performed through appropriately defined interfaces to ensure the proper understanding and use of the data.

- To enable data sharing, the data governance team, with the cooperation of the data domain stewards and the business areas, must develop, abide by, and communicate a common set of definitions, policies, and standards. Common data definitions form the foundation for systems interfaces and data exchanges. A common vocabulary increases the value of the definitions.

PRINCIPLE 3: MANAGE DATA TO FOLLOW INTERNAL AND EXTERNAL RULES AND REGULATIONS

Avoid Risk and Compliance Issues

RATIONALE

- Current legislation and regulations require the safeguarding, security, and privacy of personally identifiable information.

- Open data sharing, managed accessibility, and the release of data and information must be balanced against the need to restrict the availability of restricted, proprietary, or sensitive information.

- Data owners, in the role of data domain stewards, are accountable for data quality, definition, security, privacy, standardization, and appropriate use of data in their domains.

IMPLICATIONS

- To improve the quality and value of data—and to avoid risk and compliance issues—accountability and rules for the definition, production, and use of data must be recorded, managed, and communicated to all appropriate parties.

- The data governance team must be responsible for recording and communicating information about an individual's accountabilities across the company.

- The data governance team must work with business areas to assure that relevant regulations are documented and communicated to impacted areas.

PRINCIPLE 4: CONSISTENTLY DEFINE AND MANAGE DATA QUALITY ACROSS THE DATA LIFE CYCLE

Right the First Time, Every Time

RATIONALE

- The quality standards for data must be well defined to identify, record, measure, and report the quality of the data.

- The quality standards will focus on measuring business process and decision-making improvements from complete, relevant, and unique data.

- Enterprise critical data must be consistently tested against the standards across the enterprise, with understood standards available to all definers, producers, and users.

- Data owners, in the role of domain stewards, are accountable for data-standard definitions and appropriate use of the standards for data in their domains.

IMPLICATIONS

- To improve data quality, the data governance team, with the cooperation of the data domain stewards and the business areas, must develop, abide by, and communicate a common set of standards.

- Common data standards are the foundation for quality systems interfaces and data use. A common place to record data standards will increase the ability to improve the quality of the data

The truth is, the simpler we stay with our concepts around data governance, the easier it is for people in our organizations to understand what data governance is all about. Please feel free to use the basic principles I've described here or derive your own as a simple way of describing the mission of a sustainable data governance program.

DATA GOVERNANCE MATURITY MODEL

Many organizations I've worked with have asked to review a version of the SEI Capability Maturity Model (CMM) applied to the discipline of data governance. Recently, the CMMI© introduced the Data Management Maturity (DMM) "to support organizations that seek to evaluate and improve their data management practices."

In the words of CMMI©, the Data Management Maturity Model (DMM) was designed to bridge the perspective gap between business and IT. It provides a common language and framework depicting what progress looks like in all of the fundamental disciplines of data management, offering a gradated path to improvement which is easily tailored to an organization's business strategies, strengths and priorities. It defines data management in specific process areas grouped by categories.

I'll align this well-known model with many aspects of the Non-Invasive Data Governance approach that has helped many organizations successfully implement data governance programs.

Consider this elegantly stated description of the Capability Maturity Model© from Wikipedia:

> *The Capability Maturity Model®, a registered service mark of Carnegie Mellon University (CMU), is a development model created after study of data collected from organizations that contracted with the U.S. Department of Defense, which funded the research. This model became the foundation on which Carnegie Mellon created the Software Engineering Institute (SEI). The term "maturity" reflects the degree of formality and optimization of processes, from ad-hoc practices, to formally defined steps, to managed result metrics, to active optimization of the processes.*

When applied to an organization's software development processes, this model allows an effective approach to improving them. When applied to the process and structure of governing data, this model may also be used to improve processes and structures. Eventually, it has become clear that this model may be applied to many other processes as well. This has given rise to a more general concept described here that's applied to many business areas.

In planning their data governance evolution in a systematic fashion, many companies use the Maturity Model to control change by determining what level is appropriate for the business and technology as well as how and when to proceed from one level to the next. Each stage requires certain investment, primarily in the use of internal resources. The rewards from a data governance program increase and risks decrease as an organization proceeds through each level of data governance.

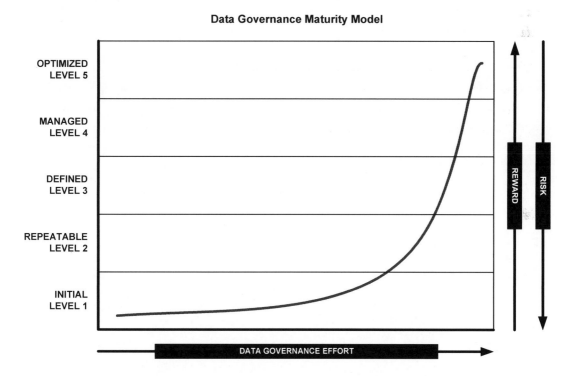

Data Governance Maturity Model

LEVEL 1 – INITIAL LEVEL

Processes at this level are typically undocumented and in a state of dynamic change. Such processes tend to be driven in an ad-hoc, uncontrolled, and reactive manner by users or events. This provides a chaotic or unstable environment for the processes.

The Level 1 organization lacks strict rules or procedures regarding data governance. Data may exist in multiple files and databases, may be used in multiple known and unknown formats, and may be stored redundantly across multiple systems by different names and using different data types. No apparent method is present in the madness, and few, if any, attempts have been made to catalog what exists. Reports are developed on the fly as requested by business units.

The quality of data in a Level 1 organization depends on the skills of technical IT analysts and developers. A Level 1 organization will take on monumental tasks with little knowledge of their impact. This causes project cancellations, or even worse, complete package implementations and updates with severely corrupted data or invalid reports, or both. About 30 to 50 percent of organizations operate at Level 1.

LEVEL 2 – REPEATABLE LEVEL

At this level, some processes are repeatable, possibly with consistent results. Process discipline is unlikely to be rigorous. Where this discipline exists, it may help to make sure existing processes are maintained during times of stress.

To move from Level 1 to Level 2, an organization must begin to adhere to data governance best practices. Best practices typically define four to six practices upon which the data governance action plan has been built.

Although Level 2 organizations follow some sort of data governance program, generally speaking, they have yet to institutionalize the program. Instead, the plans of these organizations rely on a central person or group to understand the issues and implement data governance reliably and consistently. This manifests itself by the creation of the data governance team function.

The success of Level 2 organizations depends on the skills of the technical analysts who manage the technical aspects of data. Although the differences between the business and technical aspects of data are usually, but not always, understood at some level, less effort is made to document and capture the business meaning of data. Little or no differentiation exists between the logical and physical data design.

Level 2 organizations begin to institute data governance practices focused on a specific type of data used for business unit reporting. Moving from a Level 1 to a Level 2 organization will incorporate restructuring specific data elements in the data warehouse.

Approximately 15 to 20 percent of organizations operate at Level 2. With successful implementation of a data governance launch, and the ability to repeat these same steps for future data governance launch-like activities, the organization will be well on its way to becoming a Level 3 organization.

LEVEL 3 – DEFINED LEVEL

This level involves sets of defined and documented standard processes established and subject to some degree of improvement over time. These standard processes are in place—that is, the AS-IS processes and are used to establish consistency of process performance across the organization.

Organizations that successfully move from Level 2 to Level 3 on the data governance maturity scale have documented and established a data governance program as a core component of their report development and data usage lifecycle. Level 3 organizations enforce and test to ensure that data quality requirements are defined and met. These organizations typically understand the business meaning of data and have created an organization-wide data governance function. They have a stated program that treats data as a corporate asset even if they don't entirely understand what this means.

The success of the Level 3 organization typically depends on the interaction between the data governance and project management functions and the proper use of tools. By contrast, Level 1 and Level 2 organizations may have tools at their disposal, but they usually don't apply them consistently or correctly. Sometimes, their tools linger as shelf ware. Level 3 organizations use tools to record and maintain data governance documentation, to automate data governance steps initiated by Level 2 organizations, and to begin proactively monitoring and tuning data governance performance. About 10 to 15 percent of organizations operate at Level 3.

LEVEL 4 – MANAGED LEVEL

Processes at this level use process metrics, and management can effectively control the AS-IS process, e.g. for software development. In particular, management can identify ways to adjust and adapt the process to particular projects without measurable losses of quality or deviations from specifications. Process capability is established at this level.

An organization can move to Level 4 only when it institutes a managed metadata solution to support its data environment. This enables the data governance team to catalog and maintain metadata for corporate data structures. A Level 4 organization also provides the information technology and end-user staff access to what data exists where within the organization, with definitions, synonyms, homonyms, and the like. The data governance team is involved at some level in all development efforts to assist in the cataloging of metadata and reduction of redundant data elements. This is always true in logical models and in physical models. This is true as appropriate for performance and project requirements. Level 4 organizations have begun to conduct data audits to gauge production data quality.

The success of the Level 4 organization depends on the buy-in of upper management to support the "data is a corporate asset" maxim. This involves treating data as they treat other assets such as personnel, finances, buildings, finished goods, etc. Advanced tools manage metadata (repositories), data quality (transformation engines), and databases (agent-based monitors, centralized consoles for heterogeneous database administration, etc.). Approximately 5 to 10 percent of organizations operate at Level 4.

LEVEL 5 – OPTIMIZING LEVEL

Processes at this level focus on continually improving process performance through incremental and innovative technological changes and improvements.

The Level 5 organization uses the practices evolved in Levels 1 through 4 to continually improve the data access, data quality, and database performance. No change is ever introduced into a production data store without prior scrutiny by the data governance team and documented within the metadata repository. Level 5 organizations continually try to improve the processes of data governance. Less than five percent of organizations operate at Level 5.

You can use the Data Governance Test coming up soon to help you to determine the level of data governance maturity in your organization.

CASE STUDY: ORGANIZATION IMPLEMENTS NON-INVASIVE DATA GOVERNANCE PROGRAM

From time to time, organizations enlist me to assess the data maturity of their organizations. This assessment indicates their readiness to implement a data governance program using the standard maturity model like the SEI's capability-maturity model. One such organization requested that a data governance maturity model, specifically built to their requirements, be used to produce this assessment.

The assessment of the organization using the maturity model indicated that although the organization showed signs of wanting to tackle data quality, metadata management, and business intelligence, severe problems existed with quality, documentation, and reporting. The organization lacked rules or procedures regarding data governance, data existed in multiple files and in databases of different formats, and data were stored redundantly across the organization. This organization, like the approximately 30 percent to 50 percent of organizations mentioned earlier, operated at Level 1 of the capability maturity model.

Since the maturity model had been developed to their specific requirements and the assessment was completed through intensive interviews with business and technical resources and validated by the highest level of their organization, support and sponsorship was offered for the initial phases of implementing a cross-organizational data governance program.

DATA GOVERNANCE TEST

This test enables you to perform a self-evaluation of your data governance programs. Testing in this way helps to focus on the things meaningful to your organization while honestly assessing how well you address your organization's needs.

The only way my Data Governance Test will be of use is to answer the questions with an honest evaluation of the present situation at your organization. When you take this test, you'll quickly discover that the questions asked are really just statements of discipline and that the answers you'll be asked to match are unlike any answers you've seen before.

This is a multiple choice test, but the catch is that you're just matching the answers I give you to the discipline statements I make, again given your circumstances. The goal of this exercise is to help you look inward to where positive aspects of your environment may be leveraged and where opportunities exist to improve governing data as a valued enterprise resource.

Before we start, you should keep these two questions in mind while you are matching the answers I provide to the statements of discipline based on the scale I provide below:

- In this day and age of increased complexities around regulatory compliance and reporting, information security, privacy, data classification, data integration, and complex transaction management, does it make sense for us to continue governing our data as we always have or should we at least consider how to effectively formalize the way we manage these data resources?

- Given that competition in our industry is fierce and every company is looking for the data- and information-based edge for a competitive advantage, does it make sense for us to continue governing our data as we always have, or should we at least consider formalizing how we manage our data resources?

If you keep these two questions in mind and honestly assess where you are on the 1-to-5-point continuum below for each of the data discipline statements, you can formulate a strategy that will help to convince your senior-most management that you should consider putting a Non-Invasive Data Governance program in place. In the scale column that follows, put rank your organization from one to five using these criteria:

- Five – We are perfect in the way we handle this aspect of governing our data.

- Four – We are doing okay in how we handle this aspect of governing our data. Although it's not perfect, it's acceptable for our purposes.

- Three – Room exists for improvement in this aspect of how we govern our data.

- Two – Significant room exists for improvement in this aspect of governing our data.

- One – We are at the point where, if we do not address this discipline, we'll be at an increasingly high level of risk around how we govern our data.

In grading each of these statements for your organization, be candid when you evaluate your present situation in terms of these discipline statements. Scoring partial points is allowed. For example, if you are somewhere between "room for improvement" and "significant room for improvement," feel free to score yourself with a 2.3 or a 2.7. I want this to be an easy test. Give yourself the benefit of the doubt, but be aware that more points are not always better. Rating yourself artificially higher may lull you into an unreasonably comfortable frame of mind and may leave you resistant to move yourself into a higher level.

I can almost assure you that somebody in your organization has responsibilities around each of these data-discipline areas. And it may not always be the same people. I can also say that just because somebody somewhere has responsibility for these things, this alone doesn't automatically increase your score. Is that person or group effective? Are they really trying with conviction? Do they have a well thought out plan?

THE DATA GOVERNANCE TEST

Data Governance Disciplines	Score
1. **Risk Management:** We manage the risks associated with our data. My organization understands the need to quickly adjust to the risks associated with data, and many of these rules are coming from outside of the organization. We have a person, a staff of people, or council (or all of the above) that focuses on understanding all levels of risk around the management of data. The person/staff/council regularly communicates information about data risk so that everybody understands risky behavior versus safe behavior in how we handle our data.	

2. **Data Compliance & Regulatory Control**: As an organization, we pay a great deal of attention to compliance and regulatory concerns around the data we collect, use, and share as part of making decisions and doing business. Somebody has the responsibility for documenting and communicating the rules to all individuals in the organization who handle these data. When we're audited, we can clearly demonstrate to the auditors that we follow the rules around the data.

3. **Information Security & Data Classification**: As an organization, we pay a great deal of attention to information security for all structured and unstructured data. We have an information security policy and/or something similar, e.g. guidelines, mandates. We feel comfortable with our ability to communicate, differentiate, and manage according to the rules associated with highly confidential data, internal-use data, and public data. People who share data in our organization also share the documented rules about that data, and we don't believe that information security is a concern.

4. **Metadata Management**: We have metadata for the most important data we manage. My organization knows what data we have, where that data resides, and how that data is defined, produced, and used in shared databases and on people's desktops. The information we have about our most important data is available to anybody who needs it. Just as important, we have identified and engaged people who have formal responsibility for the definition, production, and usage of metadata.

5. **Data Quality Management:** Our organization continually focuses on data quality. We have formal means for recording data quality issues, and we have proactive and reactive methods to find issues and address them when we find them. And we have people responsible for managing the issue logs, putting values to the issues and prioritizing the issues. Most important, we have a clear understanding about the business standards for core pieces of data that make it easier to differentiate high quality from low quality data.

6. **Business Intelligence and Data Integration:** We have a data warehousing environment that takes full advantage of the data therein and is used to its fullest capability. This means that people have easy access to the data, they understand the data, and they help us to continually improve the quality of the data. We recognize that data governance plays an important role in the success or failure of our data warehousing initiative on all sides of the data integration equation. We understand that data integration is a difficult discipline. But since we govern the data well on both sides—source and target—we feel

comfortable with the effective nature of our business intelligence program.	.
7. **Master Data Management:** Our organization recognizes that master data management (MDM) is one of the most effective and most important data disciplines talked about today. We've identified people to manage our MDM initiative(s) and have started to identify the enabling technologies that will help us manage and share our master and reference data. When we populate our MDM environment, the discipline is there to manage the decision-making around the master data resource, the metadata component, and the communications and accessibility to the master data. We are positioned well to complete the master data initiative within budget and on schedule.	
8. **Data Governance & Data Stewardship:** Last but not least, we have a data governance program that clearly defines roles and responsibilities at the operational, tactical, strategic, and support levels. Our program focuses on leveraging the existing knowledge of the data that lies within our data stewards. The approach we've taken has been embraced by our leadership, stewards, business, and the technology individuals and it addresses the governance of data in a proactive and reactive sense. Our data governance program is a primary contributor to our success in all of the disciplines listed in this test.	

HOW TO EVALUATE YOUR SCORES

It would be valuable for you to analyze your own scores and how you matched the five-point scale/answers to each of these discipline statements. Each of the eight areas of the data management discipline stands to be evaluated on its own. You may want to consider evaluating your organization the same way with these additional disciplines: data modeling, data mining, service-oriented architecture, cloud computing, software as a service, data mash-ups, big data, or whatever the next big thing is in data management. All of these may be included as a discipline in this test and evaluated in the same manner.

The following result breakdowns are next steps in data governance—or any single discipline—that you want to take for your organization.

- If you scored above 4, your organization is in much better shape than most. It's important to identify what you're doing well and what areas need improvement. Continue to assess what you're doing well and spend plenty of time adjusting the ship and responding to changes in the landscape.

- If your score lies between 3 and 4, your organization is still in pretty good shape. Again, it's important to recognize where you have room for improvement. I suggest that you define best practices around the areas that need improvement, leverage things you're doing well, and address head on the opportunities to improve as your organization has likely already recognized and addressed deficiencies in governing data.

- If you scored between 2 and 3, your organization is ripe for putting a Non-Invasive Data Governance program in place. Because you state that room exists for improvement, it may make sense to identify and articulate those areas that need improvement and to develop an action plan and a communications plan to specifically target these areas.

- If your score is between 1 and 2, your organization is due for a Non-Invasive Data Governance program. In fact, if you've not already started to define your data governance program, your data may likely continue to be a deficit to your organization rather than an asset.

WHAT TO DO WITH THIS INFORMATION

You'll notice a wide gap between the scale/answer that yields five points and the scale/answer that yields one point. At the higher end of the scale, little or no work needs to be done around data governance and the data disciplines listed in this test. Some of you may get results that vary widely across the eight data disciplines. If that's the case, focus your attention on improving the numbers with low scores and concentrate on bringing up your overall average.

If you're at a company that yields a 3 or lower for all categories, you have significant work to do:

- Identify a specific data discipline(s) from the test results that require immediate attention.

- Identify specific business-value points you can make about the deficiencies in the data disciplines that interfere with your organization's ability to drive value in that discipline.

- Identify industry-proven best practices for data governance as they specifically apply to that data discipline or disciplines.

- Assess your organization's present practices in comparison with the best practices to identify leverageable components and opportunities to improve.

- Articulate the gap that exists between present practices and best practices, the risks associated with that gap, and the potential value to your organization.

- Develop and deploy a proven framework of Non-Invasive Data Governance roles and responsibilities.

- Use this information to deliver an actionable work plan and an actionable communications plan to address data governance in relationship to the data discipline or disciplines.

- Gain value from working with someone who has been down this path before.

You may have found that attempting to sell the need for an over-arching, end-to-end, global, world-wide enterprise data governance program is a large pill to swallow for you as the seller or the sellee of a data governance program. If that's the case, you may want to start by putting a Non-Invasive Data Governance program in place that specifically and consistently addresses the data-discipline areas most in need and of greatest interest to your organization.

Keep in mind the overall needs of the enterprise and partner with other existing data governance initiatives or similar initiatives like security, protection, and quality improvement. At some point, you may reach a convergence of good ideas, and the overall needs of the organization will be easier to reach.

TEST CONCLUSION

You may look at this as just another self-help test. I hope not. With this test, I set out to accomplish a simple way of self-evaluation that connects the specific data disciplines identified in the test with your present state of ability to achieve value or avoid the risks associated with that discipline.

As I stated earlier, people in your organization likely have a specific interest in one or more of the data disciplines listed here. They may have more than interest; they may have accountability. Help them to help your organization to proceed and succeed with data governance. Introduce them to the Non-Invasive Data Governance approach and the results of this test. Doing so will hopefully provide you with the message you need to start down a path to success.

Key Points

* These are the four principles of data governance:
    o Data comprise an asset.
    o Data must have clearly defined accountability.
    o Data must follow rules and regulations.
    o Data should be managed consistently.

* The five layers of the data governance maturity model closely resemble the five levels of the Strategic Engineering Institute (SEI) Capability Maturity Model:
    o Level One – Initial
    o Level Two – Repeatable
    o Level Three – Defined
    o Level Four – Managed
    o Level Five – Optimizing

* The Data Governance Test enables you to perform a self-evaluation of your data governance programs for these eight disciplines:
    1. Risk Management
    2. Data Compliance and Regulatory Control
    3. Information Security and Data Classification
    4. Metadata Management
    5. Data Quality Management
    6. Business Intelligence and Data Integration
    7. Master-Data Management
    8. Data Governance and Data Stewardship.

Chapter 5
Best-Practice Development and Critical Analysis

In his book *The 7 Habits of Highly Successful People: Powerful Lessons in Personal Change*, Stephen Covey emphasizes to "begin with the end in mind" as one of the habits. Starting with the end in mind isn't just a habit of highly successful people; it's also a habit of successful organizations.

Look at it this way: It makes sense to build an action plan before you try to accomplish anything. Mapquest.com can give you directions only if you begin with the end in mind and tell it where you are heading. When building an action plan for a data governance program, it makes sense to map out what you want to accomplish, what the future state will look like, and the future behaviors of the organization. All of which brings us to data governance best practices.

Data governance best practices form the basis and guideline for the execution of a data governance program. Organizations that successfully implement data governance programs begin by defining a limited series of best practices. Once they define their best practices, they complete a gap-risk assessment to identify the differences (gap) between what they define as data governance best practices and present practices and the current and potential risks associated with the gap. Just as important, they define an action plan for delivering the data governance program.

DEFINE BEST PRACTICES

When defining best practices, use these two criteria to determine if something is a best practice for your organization:

1. *Is the best practice practical and possible to implement given your situation?*

2. *Will the program be at risk if the best practice isn't accomplished?*

You *must* be able to answer "yes" to these two questions for the practice to be considered a best practice. Keep this in mind as you read the few sample best practices below. Consider whether or not these sample questions would be answered "yes" by your organization. Perhaps the sample best practices could be considered best practices for your organization.

SAMPLE BEST PRACTICES

The examples below of best practice statements occur repeatedly with organizations across industries:

- For data governance to be successful, senior management supports, sponsors, and understands the activities of the data governance team, the roles defined in the data governance operating model, and specific examples of where data governance will add value.

- Staff members are committed to the definition, development, execution, and sustainability of the data governance program on a continual basis.

- Data governance principles are applied consistently and continuously to data that are defined, produced, and used for enterprise reporting.

- The goals, scope, expectations, measurements of success, and roles and responsibilities of the data governance program are well defined and communicated with information technology, strategic business units, and shared corporate functions.

Think about these statements in terms of the criteria shared in the Best Practices section. For the first sample best practice, you might ask, "Is it practical and doable that we can get the high level of senior management to support and understand data governance?" For the first best practice you would also ask, "Will our data governance program be at risk if we don't have senior management's support and understanding?"

The answer to these questions should be "yes." It's possible to educate senior management. Just as important, you place yourself at risk if you don't have senior management's support. These two criteria are important in the definition of data governance best practices for your organization.

PERFORM DISCOVERY BY CONDUCTING INTERVIEWS AND MEETINGS

It's important to review the best practices and to see where your organization stands in comparison with them, especially with business and technical people within your organization. The best way to complete this discovery process is through interviews and question-and-answer sessions with a fair representation of business management people who'll be identified as data stewards and IT management.

Distribute your best practices to the appropriate people before meetings to offer them an opportunity to form an opinion, whether positive or negative. Remember that best practices should be easy to understand and agreed upon. Doing so will provide a good starting place for your meeting and will reduce the time needed for the meeting.

It's important to note that if you write best practices so that people can answer "yes" to the questions, you'll likely get suggestions on how to reword the practices instead of negative feedback. The best practices should be no-brainers to understand and agree to. It is often helpful to include the three questions when you distribute the best practices for review before the meeting.

During your meetings, ask participants to tell you what they believe the organization or their parts of the organization are presently doing that supports the best practices. Also, ask them what they believe is impeding the ability to follow the best practices and where room exists for reasonable opportunities to improve. This will feed into the next steps of the assessment.

RECORD STRENGTHS

This seems rather obvious, but it's worthy of a brief mention. Leveraging the strengths you find in the discovery step is important. The focus is to identify and record activities of stewards and processes that support the best practices you've defined for your organization. The recording aspect is critical because:

1. You can use the recorded strengths as a solid starting point. If people are already performing the role of data steward, let's not change that. Where processes support the defined best practices, let's not change

these either. The list of strengths can be a starting point for discussion with people who'll become data stewards and to assure people that they needn't feel threatened by future data governance behavior.

2. Recordings of the strengths can demonstrate and sell senior management that a basis of data governance is already in place and that the action plan—the last step—won't change things that need not be changed. As the English author and politician Lucius Cary, Second Viscount Falkland, once said, "When it is not necessary to change, it is necessary not to change."

RECORD OPPORTUNITIES TO IMPROVE

The term "opportunity to improve" is often considered the politically correct way to describe "weaknesses in our present environment." Actually, it says more than that. Opportunity to improve articulates the specific areas to address that don't align with the best practices you've defined. Recording areas where improvement is necessary will play an important role in the development of your action plan. And your action plan will consist of the steps to follow to address opportunities to improve.

REPORT THE GAPS

This is another important step. Use the information collected and recorded in the previous two steps to report the gap between your present environment and the best practice environment communicated earlier. This may seem obvious, but because some companies seem to prefer the ready-fire-aim approach, I thought this worth mentioning.

Make certain to report the gaps in a positive way. Certainly, make mention of the specific strengths in this report, and sell the idea that taking advantage of the opportunities mentioned in the previous step is exactly that—opportunities for your organization to become better at managing its data.

REPORT THE RISKS

This is another, critical step. Most senior managers will quickly focus on risks, and these may likely be what they first want to assess: "Where are the gaps in our risk management program? In the areas of compliance? Security? Privacy? Identity theft? Record retention? Disaster recovery?"

Knowing where you organization is at risk, or even speculating where your organization might be at risk, can be an important contributor to the questions you ask of the business and technical people in your organization during the discovery step. This can also be a major contributor to the effort to sell senior management on the key concepts of data governance and the need to formalize a data governance program.

PREPARE THE ACTION PLAN

At this point, you've defined data governance best practices for your organization and have identified what you're doing to support the best practices. You've identified the opportunities for your organization to improve, reported the gaps between where you are and where you are going, and articulated the risks associated with the gaps. The action plan should practically write itself, right?

Well, it's not necessarily that easy. The action plan should include doable steps that address the opportunities to improve. These steps should be prioritized, communicated, and resourced. Consider tying the planned steps back to the rest of the assessment report.

The action plan should be written to accentuate the positive. Your organization should be able to achieve the action plan given the present, resource situation, and activities of your organization. The action plan must be communicated to the stakeholders in the governing of data in your organization—basically everybody. The action plan must be followed, and the results of following the plan must be communicated as well.

FINAL THOUGHTS ON BEST PRACTICES

As I mentioned in the opening paragraphs of this chapter, it's smart to begin with the end in mind. Best practices establish the beginning and the end. They set practical target behaviors that the organization must achieve for the data governance program to become a sustainable success.

Keep these three tips and techniques in mind for establishing best practices and completing the critical analysis and assessment:

1. **Do not mince words**. Organizations following the non-invasive approach to data governance purposely minimize the number of words they include in each best practice. Be sure to eliminate fluff words or words that deflect from the real meaning of each practice. Some organizations focus on the task at hand, such as protecting data, improving quality, or improving analytics, when they define their best practices.

2. **No time like the present**. Writing in the present tense is the most effective way to describe best practices. That's because each best practice is a present-state benchmark for beginning your assessment and should describe the practice the organization sets out to achieve. A best practice written in the future tense, including words like "to," "will," or "must," describes a future behavior that implies the best practice is not being followed at the present time. Earlier in the chapter I stated that to follow the Non-Invasive Data Governance approach, the assessment must first articulate present, leverageable activities (strengths) that support the best practice before articulating the opportunities to improve (weaknesses).

3. **Underline to underscore**. Best practices are often the tool used to introduce an organization to the behavioral aspects of the Non-Invasive Data Governance approach. In introducing this approach, unfamiliar words are used in communicating to the people of the organization. A best practice critical analysis and assessment should define these terms in simple language that the business and technical communities understand. Consider underlining the words in the best practices that

may be new to those who read the best practices and assessment. Provide a glossary of these underlined terms.

Key Points

- The steps to a best practice assessment include:

    o   Define best practices.
    o   Perform discovery.
    o   Record strengths.
    o   Record opportunities to improve.
    o   Report the gaps.
    o   Report the risks.
    o   Prepare the action plan.

- There are two criteria for determining if something is a data governance best practice for your organization:

    o   Is the best practice practical and possible to implement given your situation?
    o   Will the program be at risk if the best practice is not accomplished?

- Remember: do not mince words, there is no time like the present, and underline to underscore.

The best way to visualize a non-invasive operating model or framework of roles and responsibilities for data governance is through the pyramid diagram below. You'll notice that I use the term "operating model." That's because the roles and responsibilities of a Non-Invasive Data Governance program play a crucial operational role in the success or failure of data governance—from best practices, to acceptability, to long-term sustainability.

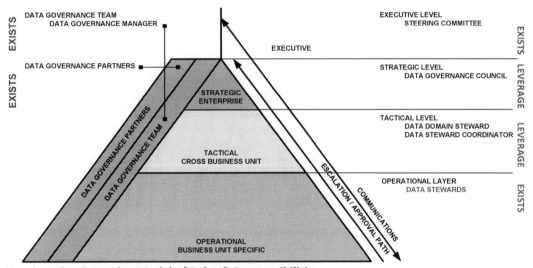

Non-Invasive Operating Model of Roles & Responsibilities

Let's start by addressing the first item that many organizations consider—the operating model. When reading the operating model of roles and responsibilities, it's best to conceive of this model in the form of a pyramid.

First, the space inside each layer of the pyramid represents the decision levels for the data. Decisions should be made at the operational level if the decisions only affect that level of the organization. This means that the majority of the decisions will eventually be made within the business areas that make up the operation level of the pyramid. Therefore, the amount of space within the operational level of the pyramid is greater than the tactical or strategic layers of the pyramid.

When decisions cross over business areas, these decisions are made at the tactical or strategic layers of the pyramid (or parts of an organization) where individuals and departments have the authority to make decisions for an enterprise regarding a certain subject area or domain of data. Examples of a domain could be customer, product, vendor, finance, or subsets of these domains or subject areas.

Many organizations find this the most difficult hurdle when developing the roles of their data governance program. At this level, the silos of data are broken down and the data are shared across business units. Finding the people to fill the roles associated with decision-making for a specific subject matter of data is not easy. Sometimes this role becomes defined through policy. At other times, this role is fulfilled at the highest level of the organization. Then the role is taken over by someone who volunteers to play the role of facilitator across business areas and who has no decision-making authority.

When this volunteer scenario becomes the case, data issues most often get escalated to the strategic layer. Note the arrows along the right side of the pyramid. One arrow represents an escalation path and the other represents the need for effective communications at all layers and roles of the operating model. The escalation path moves from the operational to the tactical and then to the strategic roles of the data governance program.

The escalation path doesn't extend into the executive layer because data issues are not typically escalated to the senior-most management of an organization. For this reason, the executive layer has no space within the pyramid. Often organizations consider that only five to ten percent of all decisions need to be raised to the strategic layer. Higher percentages often reflect difficulties of facilitating toward acceptable solutions at the tactical layer.

WHERE SHOULD DATA GOVERNANCE RESIDE?

If you've considered defining, developing, and deploying a data governance program at your company, you've probably asked the question:

Where should data governance reside?

This usually draws two responses—"in the business" or "in IT." When I ask this question, the answer I hear most often is "in the business." I wish it were that simple.

What exactly does it mean for data governance to sit "in the business"?

- By stating that data governance fits in the business, are we saying that business should manage the program? Possibly. It's also possible for an IT area, with proper cooperation and coordination with the business areas, to manage a successful data governance program.

- Are we saying that all of the data stewards should be in the business? Well, not exactly. The IT area also has data needs to manage and has data stewards for technical and tactical metadata and potentially for business data.

- Are we saying that since business "owns" the data, its members are responsible for data quality? Well, kind of. In fact, the organization really owns the data, and the business areas should take significant responsibility to be good caretakers and sharers of the definition, production, and usage of the data to improve quality, understandability, and decision-making capabilities.

When I'm asked if data governance should reside in the business areas or the IT area, I always answer "yes." Data governance should reside in both. The discipline of data governance will not be effective if managed in business areas without coordination and cooperation with the IT areas.

The same is true in reverse. Data governance is typically a universal thing. Data governance is a cross-organization and organization-wide initiative that requires barriers between IT and business to be brought down and to be replaced with well-defined roles and responsibilities for the business areas and for the technical areas of an organization. The question of who does what and when is more important than where.

Which Part of the Business?

This is a simple question. But the answer is not so simple. Data governance being "in the business" brings on more questions. Once it's determined that the data governance program will be managed in the business, if that's what an organization decides, the next question is, "Which part of the business?" Should the area responsible for compliance run the program? How about the enterprise risk area or the legal department or the finance department or the human resources area, and so on and so on? You can see that a simple answer doesn't exist to the question of which area.

The best consulting answer to the question of which area is "it depends." A good consultant will always follow that question with the statement, "It depends on..." My list, in question format, of what it depends on is this:

- Do the selected business area and the management of that area have the respect of the other business areas and IT areas and the management of these areas?

- Does this area have the ability to gain cooperation and coordination of other business and IT areas and the management of these areas?

- Does this area have the ability to put the data wellness of the organization in front of the interests of their own business area?

- Do the business area and the management of that area have responsibility for priority cross-business area activities such as Enterprise Resource Planning (ERP) implementation, data warehousing, customer data integration, and master data management?

You'll note that I've not used terms like "have authority" and "are empowered" in these questions. I did this for a reason. These terms represent all that's *unproductive* in answering the question about who'll be responsible for managing the data governance program.

These phrases raise the perception that the business area managing the program will tell people what to do, how to do it, and be ranked as the decision-making body of the program. From my experience, this could not be further from the truth. The potential or likelihood of a single business unit being empowered for an organization may not be a reality for your organization and the perception that a single business area will have the authority over the rest of the organization can ruin the possibility of success for a data governance program. In practical non-invasive data governance solutions, no single, business area can have the authority or can be empowered over the rest of the organization. Again, think back to the basic concept of coordination and cooperation.

Authority and empowerment are still important words for a data governance program. The words "authority" and "empowerment" should be defined into the data governance organization, particularly when speaking in terms of a data governance council. This body includes representatives of each business area and IT that has the authority and is empowered to make decisions on a cross-business area and strategic basis.

SHOULD DATA GOVERNANCE RESIDE IN INFORMATION TECHNOLOGY (IT)?

I've worked with several clients that started their data governance programs in IT. One company focused on running its IT area as a business unit. This company intended to manage all of IT's data including metadata, data about hardware, software, configuration, licenses, phones, data security, and login IDs. The company implemented a data governance program within the IT area to become more disciplined in how it managed IT's data - data governance for IT and managed by IT.

My point here is that there's no need to limit the governable data just to business data. And data stewards can be in the IT area. Data, not even IT data or metadata, will not manage themselves.

A large financial institution initiated an enterprise-wide data governance program managed by IT. Data governance was accepted weakly by business leaders of the organization. But the consensus was that the IT area did *not own the data*. This precipitated a well-thought-out transition of the program from the management control of IT to the management control of the enterprise risk area. This company agreed that the placement of the data governance program wasn't the overriding factor. Both agreed that the design of the data governance organization, the use of the data governance council, the ability to get people across organizational boundaries to coordinate their efforts and cooperate in proactive and reactive data governance processes were the most important factors.

LEADERSHIP IS MOST IMPORTANT

The best answer to the question "Where should data governance fit into our organization?" is this: It doesn't matter. An organization's data governance can succeed when managed either by a business area or an IT area.

Of course, the decision of which area will manage the data governance program can be important to the success of the program. It will not, however, make or break the likelihood of success of a well-defined data governance program. As long as the business and IT areas coordinate their efforts, use a data governance council as a strategic resource, cooperate in strategic data management activities, and act in the best interests of the organization data-wise, the placement of the management of the data governance program is not the most important question to be answered. When attempting to identify the best person to lead your organization's data governance program, you have two options. You can promote from within or hire from the outside.

PROMOTING FROM WITHIN

An insider with existing levels of business relationships and thorough knowledge of the data and inner workings of your organization should be considered first to run your data governance program. This person, with consultative mentoring from someone who's often traveled down this path, can leverage his or her knowledge and relationships while having access to the deep knowledgebase, the experience, and the skill of adapting components successfully within a multitude of circumstances and cultures.

Typically, a person with detailed levels of internal business knowledge and relationships can become well versed in administering data governance. This is the most effective person to run a successful and sustainable Non-Invasive Data Governance program for your organization.

HIRING FROM OUTSIDE

An outsider with experience implementing data governance in another organization should be the first person to tell you that data governance programs work best when defined, designed, developed, and deployed specifically to operate within the culture of an organization. Knowing the components of how to deploy a data governance program are critical to the success of the person in this position.

But this doesn't ensure that an outside person's prior methods will work in your organization. Not knowing your organization's data nuances or how they're managed or not managed, not knowing existing levels of accountability for business data, and not having established working relationships with the business and technical areas of your organization will put this person at a disadvantage.

Key Points

- The first and most fundamental question organizations ask about setting up the roles and responsibilities of a data governance program is *where should the data governance program reside?*

- Many organizations believe that data governance will be successful only if the program resides in a business area. This is a misconception.

- There are factors to consider in selecting the right person to lead the data governance program, and there are pros and cons of hiring from within versus promoting from the inside.

Chapter 7
Roles and Responsibilities – Operational Layer

In this chapter, I will start walking through the layers of the Operating Model where people in business areas take on the appropriate levels of accountability associated with the different roles of the model. In other words, this chapter will begin the layers of the pyramid diagram from the bottom up, starting with the different types of data stewards at the operational layers.

Chapter 7 addresses the Operational Layer of the Operating Model. The operational data stewards are located in this layer.

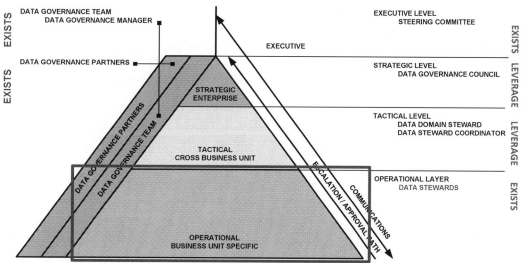

Non-Invasive Operating Model of Roles & Responsibilities with Operational Layer Highlighted

OPERATIONAL DATA STEWARD

If you subscribe to the Non-Invasive Data Governance approach, operational data stewards already exist throughout the organization. If this is new to you, please reread prior information to gain a better understanding of why and how I call the Non-Invasive Data Governance approach non-invasive. As part of their daily routines and work efforts, operational data stewards have some level of responsibility, though not necessarily authority, over data they define, produce and use.

Several years ago, the CIO at a state government organization said to me:

> *If you can see the data, you have responsibility for how you use the data you can see. If you can update the data, you have responsibility for how you update or enter the data. If you define the data that's used by your part of the organization, you have responsibility for making certain it is consistent with the standard way we define that data.*

This simple statement perfectly describes how an operational data steward becomes an operational data steward.

RULES FOR BECOMING A DATA STEWARD

I was recently asked if everybody in an organization is an operational data steward. One could argue that the answer is "yes" because everyone, at some time, comes in contact with data or uses data as part of their everyday jobs. Formally engaging or providing data awareness to everybody in the organization is not a bad idea. But formally engaging everybody in the same way is not a good idea. Let me explain.

A DATA STEWARD CAN BE ABSOLUTELY ANYBODY

If you follow or believe in the Non-Invasive Data Governance approach, you may have heard me say that you cannot tag each data steward, say "You're it," and expect him or her to start doing steward stuff. That's not the way it works.

But I do say that each person who defines, produces, and uses data in your organization has a certain level of accountability or responsibility for how data are defined, produced, and used. Persons on the front line have accountability for entering data appropriately and accurately; persons who define data have accountability for making certain they're not redefining something that's been defined before. And certainly, individuals who use data have accountability for how they use data.

The problem is that right now, these levels of accountability are often informal, inefficient, and ineffective when it comes to the necessary levels of accountability that comprise a successful environment for governing your data.

Again, this is the main concept of the Non-Invasive Data Governance approach. If we can just formalize the accountability of these stewards of data and can convince management and the stewards that they, for the most part, already govern data, doing so will make communications with everybody from senior management on down much easier to digest. I can already hear data stewards saying, "Do you mean I already do this stuff?" Of course, your response would be, "Yes. We just want to put some formality around some of the things we already do." And their response would be, "Oh, okay, I think I get it now."

BEING A DATA STEWARD DESCRIBES A RELATIONSHIP TO DATA, AND IS NOT A POSITION

If you ask me, being a data steward is neither a position nor a title. Being a data steward describes a relationship between a person and some data, whether these data are a data element, data set, subject area, application, database—however granular you want to get with your association of steward to data.

Those who define data as part of their jobs should have formal accountability for making certain they record and make available a sound business description of the data they define. Or perhaps they should have accountability for identifying and using data that already exist somewhere else. Or they should have accountability to get the appropriate people involved in the efforts to define the data.

This person can be associated with Business Intelligence (BI), Customer Relationship Management (CRM), Enterprise Resource Planning (ERP), Master Data Management (MDM), big data, package implementation, or data in the cloud effort where new data are defined for an organization. The Non-Invasive Data Governance approach calls for data definition stewards to become formally accountable for the quality of data definition.

Those who produce data as part of their jobs should have formal accountability for making certain that data are produced following the business rules, hopefully recorded, for these data. Or perhaps they should have accountability for making certain that the data they produce are entered into the system or wherever in a timely manner. Or they should have accountability for making certain that appropriate people are notified when data are updated, when data accuracy provides low levels of confidence, or when data haven't been received. This individual can be a data entry person, a data integrator, a data analyst, a report generator, or a person involved in any of the efforts described in the above paragraph. The Non-Invasive Data Governance approach calls for data production stewards to become formally accountable for the production of data.

And this leaves the data usage stewards. Everyone who uses data in a job should be held accountable for how he or she uses that data. This means that the data governance program should focus early on recording and making available the rules—regulatory, compliance, classification, and any risk management effort—associated with data usage.

The data usage steward should be held formally accountable for individuals with whom data are shared. The data usage steward should be accountable for securing and protecting the data according to the recorded and available rules. This person could be anybody in the organization who uses data for his or her job. This can be anyone.

Does this mean we need to physically record every single individual in the organization who has a relationship to data? Well, probably not. Do we need to know every division, department, and group that defines, produces, and uses the data? Probably so. Please see in Chapter 11 a copy of a Common Data Matrix spreadsheet tool I developed and have used repeatedly with organizations to help them formally record who does what with specific data across their organizations.

Being a data steward (whether as a definer, producer, or user of data) and the formal accountabilities inherent with being a data steward all comes down to each individual's relationship to data. A data steward may have two or three of the three relationships to data and may then have greater levels of formal accountability. Again, anybody can be a data steward.

A DATA STEWARD IS NOT HIRED TO BE A DATA STEWARD

I've seen organizations post full-time-equivalent (FTE) jobs for data stewards. I think this is a mistake for most organizations. As you can tell from my rules thus far, I think that data stewards already exist in your organization and they can be anybody.

I make this a rule because the people in your environment are already the stewards of data even though they may not formally consider themselves as such. Stewards are not hired unless you are hiring into other positions, and the mere fact is that any position probably defines, produces, or uses data as part of its responsibilities.

In my Operating Model of Roles & Responsibilities, I differentiate between operational data stewards, described in the previous rule, and data domain stewards at the tactical level. The data domain steward typically has a level of formal accountability, or sometimes authority, to make decisions for a specific domain or subject area of data for an entire organization or whatever part of the organization falls under the auspices of the data governance program.

Some organizations designate the data domain stewards through formal guidelines and policies. A Big Ten University I recently worked with focused on data classification as the primary driver of its data governance program. The classification policy spelled out that the registrar was the data trustee— another name for data domain steward—of student data, that the controller was the trustee of financial data, and the vice president of human resources was the trustee of employee (staff) data. This way of doing things is becoming more typical then we may think.

It makes sense for organizations to spell out, by position in the organization, the persons who hold the responsibilities of the data domain steward. In some organizations, this position is not the know-all and be-all authority on that subject matter of data. Yet this person is held in high enough regard across the organization to make certain that the data in his or her subject matter is governed properly.

In a situation where the data domain steward is not the authority or person who can make decisions for the organization, it becomes the responsibility of the Data Governance Council at the strategic level to make these decisions. It's been my experience that decisions about data are rarely escalated above the council level to the executive level.

A DATA STEWARD DOESN'T NEED THE TITLE OF DATA STEWARD

If everybody is a steward of data, then there's no reason to change people's job titles. Wouldn't doing so get confusing? As I stated earlier, any person with any title may be a steward of data. Therefore, and to stay less invasive, we should allow individuals to retain their original titles and educate them on the formal accountabilities that accompany their relationships to data. In most cases, this won't mean a major work shift for data stewards. This doesn't mean there'll be no work shift, only that it won't be a redefinition of their position or what they do.

The same probably holds true for the data domain steward. A controller need not be called the Finance Data Domain Steward and a registrar doesn't have to be called the Student Data Domain Steward. It's most important that these individuals are recognized as the persons filling the role of the data domain steward.

A DATA STEWARD DOESN'T HAVE TO BE TOLD HOW TO DO HIS OR HER JOB

A great debate is going on over whether or not data stewards need to be told how to be data stewards and whether or not data stewards can be certified as data stewards. The answer to both considerations is that it depends. Well, what does it depend on?

In my experience, data stewards don't have to be taught how to be data stewards. Rather, data stewards can be educated on the formalities of their existing relationships to data. A person who uses data must be educated on what data mean, where data came from, how data may and may not be used, how data may or may not be shared, etc. A person who produces data must be educated on the impact of how data are entered and the guidelines for the production of those data. I think you get my point.

In some ways, you could say that data stewards need to be told what this formality means and how to be the best data stewards they can be. Then the question becomes, "Does this mean we need to tell data stewards how to do their jobs?" And to that, I say a resounding "No!" We don't have to teach data stewards how to do their jobs.

PUBLIC OR INDUSTRY DATA STEWARD CERTIFICATION IS A LOAD OF BUNK

This is the second half of the answer to the questions raised by the previous rule. I firmly believe that data stewards can't be certified. Every data steward has a different relationship with data and, therefore, a different responsibility, some with formal accountability and some without.

I know some industry organizations focus on coming up with the credentials to become a certified data steward. But I'm against this idea.

I'm not against a practitioner organization or a company setting up credentials and training internally for their stewards to certify them in their positions as a steward of the specific data that define, produce, and use. Please understand this distinction. Organization certification, yes. There are well-documented cases of organizations certifying their own data stewards. Industry certification, no.

To have an industry group certify data stewards would be like telling them how to do their jobs. And you already know that this subject is covered by the previous rule.

You may tell me that data stewards could be educated but not certified on the types of activities that go with their relationship to their organization's data. This may include everything from how to access metadata and business rules about data to the formal processes that must be followed to the method of getting something approved, changed, communicated, or retired. I just have a hard time understanding how someone outside an organization and culture can provide this level of industry data steward certification.

To summarize these points, let me state again that data stewards need to be educated on the formal accountabilities that go with their relationship to data. This education may include information security and operational data rules, compliance and regulatory rules, standards and processes that have been defined—if not, they need to be—for their relationship to data.

So therefore I say "bah humbug" to industry-level data steward certification. And I make it one of my rules for being a data steward.

MORE THAN ONE DATA STEWARD EXISTS FOR EACH TYPE OF DATA

I can't tell you how many times I've begun working with an organization where a number of people point their fingers at individuals and say, "Jim, he is our Customer Data Steward." And "Mary, over there, she's our Product Data Steward." And "Mike is our Employee Data Steward."

Identifying people this way is not right. At least not if you follow any of the rules I've outlined above. Please remember that in the Non-Invasive Data Governance approach, the idea that only one data steward per type or category or subject matter is invalid. That is, unless you are talking about data domain stewards who could be given the role of the Customer Data Domain Steward, Product Data Domain Steward and so on. These people have accountability across business areas. Do not forget to insert the word *domain* or *subject area* into the role title, just to define more clearly the responsibilities of the role.

The truth is that there are many data stewards for practically every type of data that exist in your organization, if you include each person who has a relationship with data. Do we need to know exactly who all these people are and call them data stewards? No. Do we need to know that there are people with a relationship to a particular type of data within a certain part of an organizational? Yes. How else will we be able to communicate with them about these data? We need to know where data stewards exist.

DATA STEWARD TRAINING SHOULD FOCUS ON FORMALIZING ACCOUNTABILITY

Rather than certifying individuals as data stewards, a data governance program should focus on educating data stewards in your specific organization about the formal accountabilities of their specific relationships to data. Definers get education on the accountabilities that go with defining data. Producers are educated on accountabilities that go with data production. Perhaps most important, users receive education on accountabilities related to using data. And individuals who actively have two of the three relationships or three of the three relationships receive data governance education on all relationships that apply to them.

And not just general education about what data stewards do. I'm talking about education that specifically pertains to the definition, production, and use of data *they* use or data *they* steward as part of their everyday jobs.

This may be scary for some organizations since they may not have the accountabilities of each relationship for each type of data defined in a way that can be shared with their data stewards. Well, this gives you a place to start with your data governance program.

If you, as the data governance program definer, haven't defined what these relationships mean, the formal accountabilities that go with the relationships, or the specific rules associated with how data domains can be defined, produced and used, how do you expect data stewards to know what to do? Again, this gives you a good place to start.

Key Points

- A data steward can be absolutely anybody.

- Being a data steward describes a relationship to data and is not a position.

- A data steward is not hired to be a data steward.

- A data steward doesn't need the title of data steward.

- A data steward doesn't have to be told how to do his or her job.

- Public or industry data steward certification is a load of bunk.

- More than one data steward exists for each type of data.

During consulting engagements, classes, or conference presentations, I often refer to the tactical layer as the biggest hurdle for organizations to get over while implementing data governance programs.

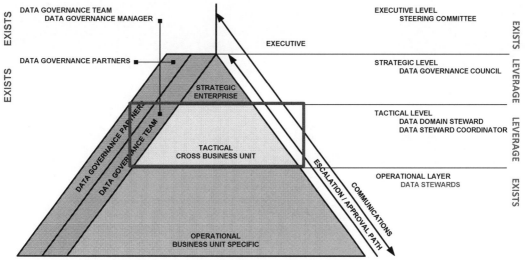

Non-Invasive Operating Model of Roles & Responsibilities with Tactical Layer Highlighted

Many organizations have become accustomed to operating in silos even though they recognize that this lies at the root of their data problems. The switch to a tactical and cross line of business (LOB), often called the "enterprise" perspective, most often brings with it pain, political battles, differences of opinion and loads of work. It's no wonder people don't want to stand in front of this train.

Identifying a position or positions that have the responsibility for the enterprise perspective for a subset of the enterprise's data can also present a challenge. To satisfy the need of managing data tactically across lines of business requires that a person in a specific position have the responsibility for that cross-LOB vision at a managed cross-operational level. This person is the data domain steward.

ENTERPRISE DATA PERSPECTIVE THROUGH DOMAINS

It should be obvious that a single person cannot manage all the cross-LOB data. Therefore, it's important to separate data that cross business units or functional areas into subsets or buckets, so to speak, of enterprise data. I refer to these buckets as domains of data. The primary responsibility of the data domain steward is to be accountable for how data in their domain are managed. This can be an important responsibility depending on the domain of data.

From my experience, there are three primary ways to spell out domains of data for an organization:

1. **By Subject Area.** This is the most common approach. The question always arises as to the appropriate level of granularity to define the domains. "Customer" may be too large and complex, while "Customer Mailing Address" may be too granular. I was recently asked, "How many domains of data will I need, and what is the typical number of domains identified in other organizations?" This isn't a simple question to answer. The answer depends on the complexity of the data and the ability to associate responsibilities with sets of data elements. Some organizations start at a higher, less granular level and break domains into subdomains or even sub-subdomains if the need arises. The lower the level of granularity, the more domain stewards. This can be a simple rule of thumb, but it doesn't necessarily mean that all domains are of the same granularity or that a data domain steward can't be responsible for more than one domain of data. Sometimes, when data doesn't perfectly slot into one subject area or another, data can be associated with more than one domain. This is not a recommended approach, but sometimes it's unavoidable.

2. **By Level-1 and Level-2 Data Resources**. This is the second-most common approach. Level 1 data resources are defined in this context as operational systems or data resources that address the needs of a single business unit or functional area. Data in Level-1 address specific operational needs and are typically referred to as "self-contained" within a business unit. Sometimes Level-1 data can be managed locally

or even at the desktop or unit server level. Level-2 systems or data resources occur when data is fed from multiple Level-1 data resources into data warehouses, data marts, Master Data Management (MDM) solutions, Enterprise Resource Planning (ERP) or package integrated data sets—anyplace where data are shared across business units or functional areas. The issue with defining domains by Level-2 data resources is that doing so often results in data falling into numerous data domains, thereby adding complexity to the data governance program.

3. **By Organizational Unit.** This approach is seldom, if ever, used. Many organizations have tried and failed to define domains by organizational units, because this approach promotes the silo and vertical view and management of the data.

The person with the enterprise perspective of a domain, typically a subject area of data, holds a pivotal role in the execution of the program. I refer to this person as the data domain steward.

DATA DOMAIN STEWARD

A data domain steward may or may not be a decision maker for a domain of data, or in general. Whether or not the data domain steward is a decision maker often depends on the position identified to be the domain steward and the responsibilities typically associated with that position. Some organizations identify data domain stewards through approved policy and anoint the defined position to be the decision makers for their domains.

Organizations on the other side of the spectrum have taken volunteers to represent the domains of data as facilitators to resolve issues around the data in that domain. There is no right or wrong answer, but one thing is certain: Organizations recognize the need to move toward the enterprise or data domain perspective.

AN AUTHORITY OR FACILITATOR?

Since there's not a single, specific level of the organization that's associated with all data domain stewards, it's difficult to state that data domain stewards are always the authoritative decision makers. Sometimes data domain stewards are in a position of authority or have the ability to break the ties between operational units. At other times, data domain stewards have less authority and become facilitators in setting standards and resolving issues with the intention of resolution across business units without escalating decision-making up to the Data Governance Council at the strategic level.

HOW DO YOU IDENTIFY A DATA DOMAIN STEWARD?

Data domain stewards typically fall within a specific line of business or business unit, and have an existing title that's something other than data domain steward. When the data domain steward acts in the domain steward role, allegiance to his or her business unit needs to be placed on the back burner. A data domain steward should have the ability to focus on the enterprise perspective rather than just the specific interests of a business unit.

The inability to act in an enterprise capacity will lead to the inability to gain the trust and support of the enterprise for decisions made or recommendations for decisions to be made coming from that position.

Data domain stewards are typically determined in one of a few ways:

- A data domain steward is the logical position or person considering the domain of data. For a university, the domain steward for student registration information may be the registrar. The director of human resources, or a designee of this position, may be a logical choice as the domain steward of HR data. The director of marketing could be the domain steward of marketing data, and so on.

- The ability to make the logical decision of the position associated with becoming the data domain steward may be more or less difficult based on how you select your domains. If it becomes difficult to identify a logical position to be the domain steward, an organization may consider breaking the domain of data into multiple subdomains that would bring with it the need for their own domain stewards.

- The domain stewards may be designated by the Data Governance Council. Sometimes, the council names the data domain stewards. This works a percentage of the time as the council looks for logical people to play the domain steward role. The selection of domain stewards may appear to be contrary to the non-invasive approach to data governance I've mentioned before. Perhaps, but recognizing such a person as a domain steward, because of his or her level of knowledge or accountability for a specific domain or subject area of data, may carry a positive connotation of increased responsibility to the organization. By assigning or recognizing someone for this role, there must be consideration for the existing work load carried by the individual selected. Giving someone responsibility who lacks the bandwidth to carry out the position can lead to an inability to manage domains of data from an enterprise perspective.

- Domain stewards may be identified by policy. I've seen organizations identify their domain stewards through verbiage in the data operations, data classification, data security, and privacy policies. Again, the authors of the policy do their best to select the logical position to carry out the data domain steward role. In any case, the existing workload of the person selected becomes important.

- Data domain stewards may volunteer for the role. I've seen individuals step forward and volunteer to be domain stewards for described domains of data. I overheard one gentleman state, "I may not know everything that's needed to be known about the domain of data, but I will do my best to facilitate acceptable standards of data within my domain and facilitate acceptable resolution of data issues pertaining to the data in my domain."

As you can see, there's no single way to identify the position that should be associated with managing a domain of data.

TRAITS OF A DATA DOMAIN STEWARD

Here is a list of personality and human traits I've found useful in identifying individuals who are appropriate data domain stewards:

- Data domain stewards should have a vision of what the future of data integration within the department can be, have the ability to get others to see the vision, and align all data-related activities with achieving the goals of the organization.

- Data domain stewards are rarely satisfied with the way data are managed. They continually look for ways to improve the status quo of how data are managed and continually strive for improvements in how data are defined, produced, and used.

- Data domain stewards should have the ability to motivate the organization to achieve data integration by including all parties interested or mandated to integrate their data.

- Data domain stewards should set an example of data-related behavior for the department. They should exhibit the data-related behavior they want from the department every day and in everything they do.

- Data domain stewards should be team players. They must develop and help achieve common goals and have a shared sense of purpose regarding their specific subject matter and its linkages with organizational goals. They should be able to draw on their own strengths, to look to others as resources, and to hold one another accountable where they are interdependent.

- Data domain stewards should be diplomatic when dealing with other stewards. Conflict is an inevitable part of teamwork, as people differ from one another, and situations are frequently ambiguous where values may differ. An inability to come to grips with conflict seriously limits a team player. Data stewards must have the personal interest, intuitive ability, and communication skills to facilitate issue resolution to achieve a win-win result.

WHAT DO DATA DOMAIN STEWARDS DO, AND WHEN DO THEY GET INVOLVED?

These two questions are perhaps the most important questions to be answered. Here are some examples of what data domain stewards do and when they get involved:

- A data domain steward gets involved when standards are being developed for data elements in the steward's data domain. This definition of standards occurs when integrating data or developing a new go-to data resource such as an enterprise data warehouse, a master data management solution, and package implementations like Enterprise Resource Planning (ERP) solutions. Getting people to agree on what data should look like moving forward is a responsibility of a data domain steward.

- A data domain steward becomes involved when resolving issues pertaining to data in his or her domain. This is often an add on to the previous bullet. Differences of opinion are inevitable when the development of data resources in the past have been marked by autonomy whether on purpose in mergers and acquisitions, or by lack of management over how data has been defined, produced and used in the past. The effort of pulling disparate data together is typically difficult when the same or similar data are defined numerous ways. The data domain steward is often in the middle of deciding how the data in the integrated data set should look and how data from the disparate sources are mapped to the integrated data set.

- A data domain steward gets involved when it becomes important to document and communicate the rules and regulations around the data in his or her domain. The data domain steward, or a designee, is the appropriate position to have the responsibility of documenting how the data in a domain are classified—open, sensitive, restricted, secured— and how the business rules around the data in a domain are audited and regulated. The data domain steward has the responsibility to make certain that this documentation is collected, recorded, communicated, and shared among all stakeholders in the data. It's no longer acceptable for a company or an employee to say, "I didn't know the rules." The government has taken care of this for us, and severe penalties and levels of risk are associated with not knowing.

- A data domain steward gets involved in new projects where data in the steward's domain is defined, produced, and used. Often these projects may take place over long periods of time. This is not to suggest that the domain steward participates in every step of these projects. Typically, the domain steward is asked to participate in activities that focus on the definition of standards and resolving cross-business unit issues pertaining to the data in his or her domain. The balance of the stewarding activities is typically left to the operational data stewards, who are the daily definers, producers, and users of data within their business units and functional areas.

The data domain steward plays a pivotal role in a successful data governance program. Identifying the data domains, identifying the data domain stewards, and enabling the domain stewards to successfully manage data across the enterprise is an early step in the development of a data governance program.

DATA STEWARD COORDINATOR

To manage or monitor the activities of the numerous operational data stewards in each unit or area, a best practice in data governance dictates that someone have the responsibility of coordinating the stewards' activities. Most often, operational data stewards won't govern themselves. As the name suggests, the data steward coordinator is a business unit or functional area responsibility for coordinating the activities of the data stewards in their units or areas.

This responsibility makes certain that stewards who define, produce, and use data are involved when they need to be in promoting healthy data activities and addressing data quality issues including:

1. Identifying data stewards in their business units/functional areas.

2. Coordinating data steward involvement in proactive and reactive data governance activities.

3. Communicating changes to data policy, regulations, and rules to the affected data stewards in their units/areas.

A data steward coordinator is often in the middle of data governance communications and data governance activities. One of the most important aspects of responsibility goes beyond traditional coordination or management of personnel activities. At several, critical points, communications tend to break down across organizations, putting the organization at unnecessary risk. The formalization of the data domain steward discussed earlier involves identifying a person or persons with responsibility for documenting, knowing, and communicating the rules around the data that are a part of their domains.

DATA DOMAIN

Stewards are responsible for recording and sharing information about changes to the data in their domains. This information may include:

- Policy – Description of and change to formal and approved manners to define, produce, and use data.

- Regulation – Description of and change to how an external entity dictates how data may be defined, produced, and used.

- Rules – Internal business specifications for how data may be defined, produced, and used.

While the data domain steward has responsibility for documenting and communicating these types of changes to the coordinator, the data steward coordinator has the responsibility for communicating the types of changes mentioned above to the data stewards in their units/areas affected by changes. This closes the loop of the communications process. The coordinator has the responsibility for communicating with the impacted people in their areas.

ASSIGNING DATA STEWARD COORDINATORS

Data steward coordinators are typically effective when their responsibilities are associated with the data stewards of their specific business units and functional areas. Therefore, the first step in identifying coordinators involves identifying the units/areas they'll represent. The responsibility of describing the units/areas for data governance purposes typically falls into the hands of the team of individuals responsible for establishing the data governance program.

The units/areas are often gathered from an organizational chart, or they can be determined by documenting the companies, divisions, departments, teams, and so on, that make up your organization. If the units/areas are defined at a company level, the company determines how granular it wants to get with defining units/areas. For example, it's not uncommon for units/areas to focus on different levels, some at units/areas at a departmental level and some at a division level.

Once the definition of units/areas has been completed, the most senior level manager of that lowest granularity group often identifies or assigns a logical person—sometimes, but not always, by position—to help coordinate the activities of the stewards in his or her group and to act as the point person for data-oriented communications.

DATA STEWARD COORDINATOR RESPONSIBILITIES

The data steward coordinator may be responsible for one, several, or all of the following responsibilities:

- Identifying the operational stewards of data per domain for their units/areas. This typically requires research and inventory time for the data steward coordinator.

- Acting as the point communications person for distributing rules and regulations per domain of data to the operational stewards in their business units and making certain that the operational data stewards understand the rules and risks.

- Acting as the point communications person for his or her business unit to document and communicate issues pertaining to specific domains of data to the proper data domain steward.

- Acting as the point person in the Common Data Matrix, or data steward repository, according to a regular change control process. A regular change control process takes place on a scheduled basis to assure that all changes that require a change to the Common Data Matrix are entered in a timely manner and on a regular basis.

- Working alongside the data domain stewards and operational data stewards on specific tactical data steward teams set up for the duration of issue resolution or project focused tasks.

- Researching exactly how and what data are defined, produced, and used in their units/areas and by whom.

Key Points

- The data steward coordinator typically has no decision-making authority but plays a pivotal role in data governance and data stewardship success.

- A data domain steward is the logical position or person considering the domain of data.

- Data domain stewards should have a vision of what the future of data integration within the department can be and have the ability to get others to see the vision.

- Data domain stewards should have the ability to motivate the organization to achieve data integration by including all parties interested or mandated to integrate their data.

- A data domain steward gets involved when standards are being developed for data elements in a steward's data domain.

- Responsibilities of data steward coordinators include identifying data stewards in their business unit/functional areas, coordinating data steward involvement in proactive and reactive data governance activities, and communicating changes to data policy, regulations, and rules to the affected data stewards in their units/areas.

The strategic layer of the Operating Model of Roles & Responsibilities pyramid represents the Data Governance Council and the Executive Steering Committee.

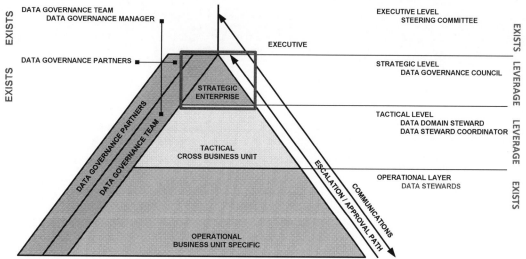

Non-Invasive Operating Model of Roles & Responsibilities with Strategic Layer Highlighted

Strategic decisions need to be made when decisions can't be made at the operational level (specific business unit) or the tactical level (first line of cross-business unit functionality) of accountability. Strategic decisions require that the people who make the decisions have the appropriate knowledge and documentation to help them to make the right decisions. This, in part, is what data governance is all about—sharing, recording and using knowledge about data.

A data-oriented strategic decision can be as major as the definition of a customer, as complex as the decision to use the coding scheme from system A or system B in the warehouse, or as involved as deciding which data profiling tool will best fit in your environment. These data-related decisions will have an impact across the organization and need to be made. Somebody (or some group) needs to be in a position to make these decisions. My suggestion, in line with many organizations defining a strategic level of data governance responsibility, is that this strategic group should be called the Data Governance Council.

DATA GOVERNANCE COUNCIL

Think of the group already used to define a strategic level of decision-making individuals in an organization. These individuals are asked to convene regularly to make decisions by representing their division, business unit, company, and so on. Could you leverage an existing group or replicate a group like that with data-savvy individuals who can understand the data governance program and step in to make decisions based on sufficient data knowledge?

ARE DATA GOVERNANCE COUNCIL MEMBERS SUPREME BEINGS?

The answer to this question is "yes" because council members serve as a kind of supreme court in matters of data governance. Typically, they are the end of the escalation line when it comes to making decisions.

We've already established that the decision-making buck stops with these individuals when it comes to strategic decisions made around the definition, production and usage of enterprise data. The fact that these people are at the strategic level implies that they may not be hands-on involved in day-to-day operations. Often, they're only as informed about the daily definition, production, and usage of data as they want to be or have time for.

Some strategic thinkers are very hands on. Some are less so. This group is typically not involved in day-to-day operations of data governance because they have vice presidents in some cases, directors, mangers, supervisors, and so on, who work for them to handle those responsibilities.

In successful data governance programs I've been involved with, only a small percentage of data-related decisions, sometimes as few as one percent, get escalated through the operational and tactical ranks to reach the Data Governance Council. By the time the decision-making reaches these supreme beings, the knowledge about the issue—cause and effect, source(s), or threat, to name a few—should be recorded and prepared for presentation in a to-the-point manner. This is the responsibility of the group that administers the data governance program (the Data Governance Team in the pyramid diagram) as well as the operational and tactical stewards involved in decision activity.

Thrones and crowns are not required at the regular Data Governance Council meetings. Often the meeting attendees are brought together through technology. As often as needed, virtual meetings can be held when an issue requires attention and a regular meeting is not close. Timely communications with the Data Governance Council requires significant attention when rolling out a program.

IS THE DATA GOVERNANCE COUNCIL THE TOP OF THE DATA FOOD CHAIN?

The simple answer to this question is, "Yes." The only level higher, the Executive Level (see the pyramid diagram), includes the sponsors and the senior-most management of the organization—the individuals who are typically far removed from daily operations and don't have time to become involved in data-oriented decisions.

The Executive Level may set priorities and may squash projects and programs they don't understand (Hint!), but the strategic-level decision-making often takes place at the next level down, at the level of the supreme beings or the Data Governance Council.

WHY DO YOU NEED A COUNCIL?

I've defined data governance earlier as "the execution and enforcement of authority over the management of data and data-related assets." Of course, this definition can be, and has been, debated in several settings. Nonetheless, there needs to be a level of authority over how data is managed. Somebody has to be responsible and accountable for making the tough decisions where the enterprise is concerned.

This group should be formal and should include all necessary parts of the enterprise. This isn't always the case. The Data Governance Council typically has representation from all areas of the business and technology. This council should be formal if its members will be expected to make strategic decisions that will impact business and technology areas. Organizations have attempted to leave the strategic decision-making to the data domain stewards at the tactical layer and have often found that these decisions need to be validated by a strategic council or committee.

This group may already exist in your organization without the data component, or with a completely different name. At a recent client, a university, the name of this group was the Administrative Systems Group. This implied IT, but it was not. Another recent client called this group the Data Council; another client called it the Technology Review Board, implying IT, and it was. Search for such a group before starting a new group.

CASE STUDY: IDENTIFYING DATA GOVERNANCE COUNCIL MEMBERSHIP

The makeup of the Data Governance Council is often easy to describe—one person per division, business unit, or however you break your enterprise down at the highest level. At the university I just mentioned, five people on its council represented the five divisions of the university—Academic Affairs, Student Affairs, and so on.

At a bank, the divisions were Human Resources, Finance, Risk Management, and so on. At a manufacturer implementing SAP, the council comprised individuals who represented four companies that were pulled together in the same SAP instance. At a government organization the council is made up of divisional representatives.

Often, I suggest that each division provide a backup or an alternate representative who may or may not have voting (decision-making) capabilities for his or her division. When the representative can't attend a meeting or become involved in a decision, the alternate has the responsibility for bringing the information forward to the council members.

HOW MUCH TIME SHOULD COUNCIL MEMBERS SPEND ON DATA GOVERNANCE?

This question of time varies for each organization. Typically, members of a Data Governance Council are asked to attend monthly or quarterly meeting of 60-90 minutes. I suggest that members allow another 60 minutes or so a month to review information shared with them by the resources implementing the data governance program. Often, their materials consist of items that have been, or will be, discussed in regular meetings. This part is easy to quantify, because members of the council can plan in their schedules and review at their convenience.

In the early phases of data governance program development and rollout, you may consider holding meetings with members of the Data Governance Council to explain the basis and drivers of the program, the key concepts, and best practices of the Non-Invasive Governance approach, the organization, the policy, and so on, so that they feel a part of the definition of the program. In some organizations, the Data Governance Council is asked to or required to approve those items just mentioned.

The difficulty of quantifying the amount of time becomes apparent when issues that are escalated to the council are being discussed and resolved. Often these issues are not resolved during the council meetings and are prioritized according to their importance to the organization. The time involved in resolving the issues can range from simply making a decision based on the information provided to them to forming working groups and committees to resolve more complex issues.

As a program matures, the Data Governance Council meets regularly with the individuals responsible for administering the program, who typically set the initial agenda. Often, the Data Governance Team Leader chairs meetings and actively engages all members of the council.

WHAT DOES THE DATA GOVERNANCE COUNCIL DO?

The Data Governance Council includes these responsibilities:

- Become interested in data governance because you recognize shortcomings in the way your organization manages data.

- Become educated in what data governance means and how it can (and will) work for your organization.

- Become educated in what it means to embrace data governance and activate your organization's data stewards.

- Approve items that need to be approved such as data policy, data role framework, methods, priorities, and tools.

- Push data governance into their areas by actively promoting improved data governance practices.

- Make decisions at a strategic level in a timely manner given the appropriate knowledge to make those decisions.

- Meet regularly (or send an alternate) and read minutes to stay informed of data governance program activities.

- Identify and approve pivotal data governance roles including cross-enterprise domain stewards and coordinators.

It can be problematic for the data governance program to overburden the Data Governance Council. As a client once told me, "These people have day jobs." The idea of the Non-Invasive Data Governance approach is to get people doing the right thing around the management of data. Sometimes this involves strict authority. At other times, it is just, "I need to know the right thing to do."

Consider leveraging your existing organizational structure to handle the responsibilities of the Data Governance Council. Also, consider limiting the number of issues that require the Data Governance Council's decisions. This second point requires additional data governance structure that exists at the tactical level.

EXECUTIVE LEADERSHIP TEAM

Much has been written about how to convince the highest level of an organization that a data governance program is necessary and how to gain management support, sponsorship, and understanding for and about it. I address the non-invasive approach for achieving this support in Chapter 1.

The Executive Level of the pyramid has no space inside the tower projecting from the top of the pyramid. Thus, this layer differs from the other three layers. Earlier, I had mentioned that data decisions are seldom escalated to the executive level of an organization. Typically, data decisions escalate to the strategic level designated or appointed by the executive level to represent their divisions in the highest level of data decision-making.

The top of the model, the Executive Layer consists of something that already exists in many organizations. That something is the executive level of management for the organization. This is the level we spelled out earlier that has to support, sponsor, and understand data governance and the activities of the program.

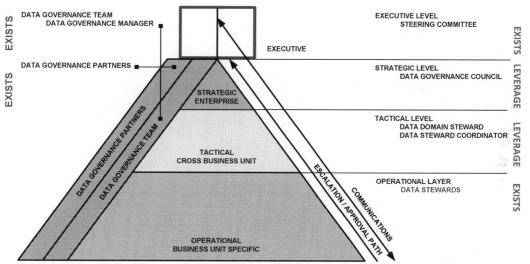

Non-Invasive Operating Model of Roles & Responsibilities with Executive Layer Highlighted

The executive layer of the operating model has no other specific function in the data governance program besides supporting, sponsoring, and understanding data governance. This section does not detail specific roles and responsibilities of the executive level because there are no responsibilities other than these three.

The data governance program will, however, risk failure if the executive level doesn't support, sponsor, and understand data governance.

Key Points

- You need a Data Governance Council because somebody has to be responsible and accountable for making the tough decisions where the enterprise is concerned. This group should be formal and should include all necessary parts of the enterprise.

- The Data Governance Council:

    o Becomes interested in data governance because you recognize shortcomings in the way your organization manages data.

    o Becomes educated in what data governance means and how it can (and will) work for your organization.

    o Becomes educated in what it means to embrace data governance and activate your organization's data stewards.

    o Approves items that need to be approved such as data policy, data role framework, methods, priorities, and tools.

    o Pushes data governance into their areas by actively promoting improved data governance practices.

    o Makes decisions at a strategic level in a timely manner given the appropriate knowledge to make those decisions.

    o Meets regularly (or sends an alternate) and reads minutes to stay informed of data governance program activities.

    o Identifies and approves pivotal data governance roles including cross-enterprise domain stewards and coordinators.

- The executive layer of the operating model has no other specific function in the data governance program besides supporting, sponsoring, and understanding data governance.

Thus far, we've discussed the overall Non-Invasive Data Governance Operating Model of Roles and Responsibilities and the portion of the pyramid operating model that falls within the pyramid and the tower projecting from the top. Now, this chapter focuses on the two shaded sidebars along the left side of the pyramid. These roles are the supporting-level roles of the model and data governance.

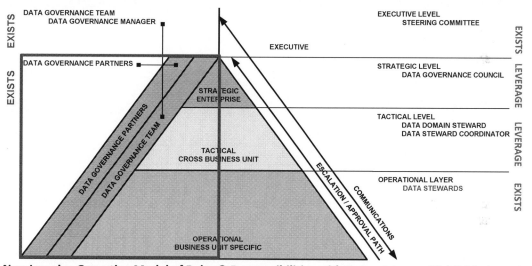

Non-Invasive Operating Model of Roles & Responsibilities with Support Layers Highlighted

It doesn't matter what your organization calls these roles or any of the roles described in the operating model of roles and responsibilities. Please don't feel as though you have to use the role names described here. It's more important that you define and communicate clearly the responsibilities described in this chapter and have the responsibility to fulfil these roles.

The Support Level of the Operating Model is represented by the two sidebars along the left side of the operating model pyramid. The Support Level includes the data governance partners and the data governance team. As stated in the chapter about best practices, the best practices call for the data governance program to be managed and administered by a data governance team, with an extended group of individuals consisting of data governance partners.

DATA GOVERNANCE PARTNERS

Data governance partners are responsible for liaising with the data governance team to provide required support, to liaise with the tactical and operational teams on data related incidents or projects, and to assure timely completion of data related requirements.

Partners may include individuals from the areas listed below. As a rule, they are specific to the organization putting their program in place:

- Information Technology.

- Regulatory and Compliance.

- Information Security.

- Project Management Office.

- Audit and Legal.

Not all of these groups may participate as partners of the data governance program and data program team. The decision to include these groups as partners may be as individual as the culture of the organization itself.

Individuals considered data governance partners participate in the data definition and standard efforts as needed, participate in the technical activities, address data concerns as needed, and champion the integration of data governance within their areas of expertise.

Data governance partners make sure that a standard project methodology is followed and that data governance activities, procedures, and metrics are in place for maintaining and improving data definition and quality of metadata. The partners see to it that metadata critical to data governance is included in the data governance documentation platform, including the data glossary and the data dictionary, and is accessible to all staff.

The amount of time commitment of data governance partners varies depending on the number of data activities defined by the data governance team, existing projects, and the requirements for data governance as part of their normal business activities.

THE DATA GOVERNANCE TEAM

Data governance team (DGT) members are individuals already employed in the organization who have a percentage of their time allotted to work toward the definition, development, and deployment of data governance in the enterprise. Notice that I didn't say that they are dedicated to data governance. Doing so implies that data governance makes up their primary responsibility, or that a larger percentage of their time is spoken for by the data governance program. In some organizations, this may in fact be the case. But in most organizations delivering a data governance program, these people have "day jobs."

Typically, the responsibilities of a data governance team (DGT) include:

- Overseeing the development and implementation of the data governance program.

- Reviewing and documenting the organization of appropriate data governance best practices, roles and responsibilities, communications and awareness plan, and providing a roadmap for the delivery of the data governance program.

- Facilitating the data governance council meetings regarding data governance status, activities, successes, and issues.

- Developing and continuously delivering data governance educational, awareness, and mentoring materials.

- Defining, recommending, and gaining approval of data governance metrics from the data governance council.

- Ensuring that data standard definitions, procedures, and metrics are in place for maintaining and improving the management of risk, quality, and usability of the enterprise data.

- Managing data incidents including missing or incorrect data reports and data access problems.

- Randomly checking on compliance with data business roles compliance.

The data governance team leader's responsibilities must include directing the activities of the data governance team members, planning, setting the agenda, facilitating, and directing data governance council meetings. The team leader ensures successful completion of actions defined for the data governance team.

It's worth noting that data governance team members are *not* the tactical or operational data stewards, and they are *not* responsible for getting existing, informal, data governance initiatives to change. Simply put, the data governance team is responsible for defining, delivering, and sustaining the activities of the data governance program. Without this team, the program will be unable to succeed.

CASE STUDIES: DATA GOVERNANCE TEAMS

A university recently developed a data governance program and had a data governance team consisting of one-eighth of one person's time. That's all. I was told that progress on the program would be slower and more tedious than normal because of this team's time constraints. In fact, progress did take a longer time.

I recommended that this team identify specific people in the organization who could play the role of confidantes for the team in matters of data issues and data governance. These confidantes became a de-facto data governance support in consideration of their interest and the time they allocated to working with the formal team consisting only of the time of one-eighth of one person.

At the opposite end of the spectrum, I assisted another organization that already had a data governance program started or partially in place. In this instance, the data governance team consisted of fourteen people. Ten were consultants from a single company; the eleventh person was the team leader from the same company; another person was from the company itself, and I served as the newest member.

The organization's business areas that sponsored the data governance program raised two questions: Why were so many people on the team, and why did it cost so much? The reason, according to the team leader, was that the data governance team's responsibilities were to fix data quality issues.

Needless to say, it was overkill to have this many people on the data governance team. As a rule, the job of the data governance team isn't to correct data quality issues. Eventually, the organization took a more appropriate approach to building its data governance team, and the responsibilities of the team changed to more closely echo the responsibilities identified in the balance of this chapter.

PROJECT TEAM VS. PROGRAM TEAM VS. PLAIN OL' DATA GOVERNANCE TEAM

Over the years, I've seen this team given several names and made up of different individuals in different roles and from different parts of an organization. In organizations just starting to put data governance programs in place that have formal support and sponsorship, sometimes this group consists of people from nearly every part of an organization. Often this group of "volun-told"—that is, told to volunteer—resources is put in place solely to define and develop the program rather than serving as part of the group responsible for the deployment of data governance.

In situations like this, the team is often referred to as the data governance project team, the project being the initial work that goes into building the program. In organizations with a program team, these individuals transition into other roles defined as part of the program. These roles range from council members to data domain stewards to operational data stewards, depending on their individual relationship to the data they define, produce, and use.

CASE STUDY: PROJECT TEAM VS. PROGRAM TEAM

A government organization recently made a clear distinction between the roles of the data governance project team and the data governance program team. The project team consisted of one or more individuals from each division of the government agency.

These individuals were actively involved in the definition of the data governance program, from best practices for that agency down to the roadmap the agency would follow to rollout and deploy the data governance program division-wide.

Understandably, the question arises: How many people should be on the data governance team? The answer is it depends. The required number of individuals on the team typically depends on:

- The level of involvement of the business areas and IT areas in the deployment of the program,

- The complexity and knowledge of the existing data management environment, and

- The speed at which organization will deploy the program.

A data governance program will not run itself. Somebody or some group needs to have the responsibilities listed above.

ROLE OF IT IN DATA GOVERNANCE

In many organizations, the information technology (IT) professionals possess a great deal of knowledge about the definition, production, and usage of data by individual business units, data used across business units, and data as an enterprise resource. It would be foolish not to leverage that knowledge to support and improve data governance across the organization. I often refer to the IT staff that has such in-depth data knowledge as the "Data Subject Matter Experts" (DSMEs) and the "System Subject Matter Experts" (SSMEs).

Data subject matter experts are individuals in IT who support the business professionals and the technical professionals with their knowledge of business operations and data necessary to operate and perform analysis of these business operations. These people may be business analysts, reporting analysts, data architects, data modelers, project managers—basically anybody in the IT area who has knowledge of the data used to support the operational business units and the enterprise as a whole.

System subject matter experts are individuals in IT who support business and technical professionals with their knowledge of the business and the software systems, internally developed applications and integrated data sets such as data warehouses, master data management solutions, and package implementations used to operate the business areas and the analytics required for decision-making within those business areas. These people can be system architects, system developers, application developers, program directors for data warehousing or Master Data Management (MDM)—basically anybody who has system oriented knowledge that supports the operational business units and the enterprise as a whole.

This distinction between the people who are DSMEs and the people who are SSMEs is trivial and not important for most organizations. What's important, however, is that the roles of the DSMEs and SSMEs become formal, to record information about these people as experts, and to use these roles to benefit an organization.

Typical Roles of the IT DSMEs and SSMEs:

- Focus on consistent protection and classification of data by data classification, e.g. confidential, public, internal use, and the like.

- Responsible for technical data handling to meet data classification requirements.

- Secure IT Infrastructure on behalf of the business units that own the data.

- Ensure that sensitive data, regardless of format, are protected at all times by using only approved equipment, networks, and other controls.

- Responsible for championing the integration of data governance within the standard project methodology.

- See to it that standard project methodology is followed and that policies, procedures, and metrics are in place for maintaining and improving data quality and the creation, capture, and maintenance of metadata.

- Ensure that all strategic data are modeled, named, and defined consistently.

- Make sure that projects source and use data as much as is feasible from the designated system of record.

- Provide technical support for assuring data quality.

- Provide technical support for data governance and data cleansing efforts where required.

- Assure that metadata critical to data governance are included in the metadata resource and are accessible.

This and the previous two chapters complete the roles and responsibilities as outlined in the pyramid diagram.

Key Points

- Data governance partners are responsible for liaising with the data governance team to provide required support, to liaise with the tactical and operational teams on data related incidents or projects, and to assure timely completion of data related requirements.

- Data governance partners may include participation from information technology, regulatory and compliance, information security, project management office, and audit and legal.

- The data governance team consists of people already in an organization who have a percentage of their time allotted to work toward the definition, development, and deployment of data governance in the enterprise.

- The data governance team is responsible for defining, delivering, and sustaining the activities of the data governance program.

Chapter 11
Data Governance Tools – Common Data Matrix

The final chapters of this book focus on simple tools, templates, and techniques you can use to make your data governance program a sustainable success. In these chapters, I introduce you to do-it-yourself tools to help you reach this goal.

I've often said that you can't buy a software tool, implement that tool, and have a data governance program. I would, however, be the first to admit that you can purchase tools to help you get started. Many tools on the market focus on assisting you to collect metadata about people's relationships to the data and make this information available to others. For that reason, all tools, purchased and the ones I describe in these two chapters, can be necessary to execute and enforce authority over the management of data.

You can use software tools to help—emphasis here on "help"—make your data governance program successful. But the tools, by themselves, won't formalize people's behaviors associated with governing data. A tool by itself isn't a data governance program. You have to know what you want the tool to do. And the large percentage of the cost of the tool will be learning how to use, populate, and maintain it.

Using a tool to collect metadata may help your program, but you can collect metadata before you purchase new software tools. I suggest that you start with homegrown tools like the ones described here and understand how these tools will help you. Whatever tool you select, it's imperative that the tool match your specifications and requirements before you purchase it.

The Common Data Matrix is a tool you can create using a spreadsheet format that is widely used by organizations implementing a Non-Invasive Data Governance plan. In fact, many of these organizations consider the Common Data Matrix their most practical data governance tool, and it is and the one they most often start with.

When I speak at conferences on data governance, I present the Common data matrix early in the presentation. Because this tool is easy to complete, it doesn't take attendees long to start filling it in. Attendees are taken with its simplicity, coherence, and practicality. To my chagrin, once I present the Common Data Matrix, they start filling it in and spend less time listening to me.

I designed the Common Data Matrix as a two-dimensional grid in the form of a spreadsheet that cross-references data of your organization with the individuals who define, produce, and use the data. Down the left side of the matrix you'll see a categorization of data domains, subject areas (or, as you might say, the buckets of data) you care about in your organization. Across the top, organizations spell out business areas, business units and lines, and divisions just as they break them out on their organization charts.

NON-INVASIVE DATA GOVERNANCE™ -- COMMON DATA MATRIX

Role Color Key		Information Technology			Corporate Unit(s)			
Data Governance Council Representative								
Data Governance Council Alternate					Area CU-1	Area CU-2	Area CU-3	Area CU-IT
Data Steward Coordinator		*samples*						
Data Domain Steward		Data/System Name	Data SME	System SME				
Operational Data Steward								
samples								
CUSTOMER DATA	VP OF OPER							
CUSTOMER ADDRESS DATA								
		ERP SYSTEM						
		MDM DB						
		EDW DB						
CUSTOMER DEMOGRAPHICS DATA								
		ERP SYSTEM						
		MDM DB						
		EDW DB						
CUSTOMER FINANCIAL DATA								
		ERP SYSTEM						
		MDM DB						

STEP 1: DEFINE DATA DOMAINS (THE ROWS)

Complete data categorizations by first defining subject areas of data meaningful to your organization. Many organizations start with domains of high level subject areas like customer, product, employee, and finance. Then spell out subdomains as different aspects (or subdomains) of products and customer like customer demographics, customer behavior, and customer preferences.

Still other organizations define their domains in a granular fashion. This includes defining core individual pieces or elements of meaningful data such as the data they feed key performance indicators or other performance metrics.

The important thing is that there are no right or wrong answers on spelling out the domains and the manner in which you define them. In fact, domain definitions look different from organization to organization.

You might ask: How granular do you need to get in defining the subject matter, the sub-subject matter, and the data? The truth is you can get as granular as your organization needs. The level of granularity is self-defined.

For example, the customer data domain includes a lot of data. Subdomains like customer demographics often include a lesser amount of more specific data spelled out, like customer street address, telephone number, and email address. Users of the Common Data Matrix identify the data and granularity they need by filling out the left side of the Common Data Matrix to meet the requirement of the data they're planning to govern.

Organizations have started down the path of defining systems or databases as the domains of data. This approach often changes quickly when organizations recognize that many of the data resources in the organization contain data from several different subject areas rather than a single subject. My suggestion is that you first start more broadly and then identify the systems or databases where the data in these subject areas reside.

Don't feel it's important to focus on all of domains of data at one time. Organizations that successfully implement data governance programs often approach their programs incrementally by starting with a single or limited number of domains rather than attempting to govern all domains of data right from the start.

If an organization uses an enterprise data model (EDM), the organization often uses the subject areas of data defined as part of that model. These subject areas are logical breakdowns of the data an organization cares about. That's why it makes sense to use the domains down the left side of the Common Data Matrix.

In comparison, defining a domain as the data warehouse typically encompasses multiple subject areas of data, and these data also reside in other data resources. This makes it more difficult to record how and where these data are represented across the organization.

Organizations have, however, used the Common Data Matrix to break down the domains and subdomains of data into data resources where these data can be found. In the shared example matrix, you can see that the customer demographic information may exist in the data warehouse, in the master data management solution, and in the enterprise resource planning package that's used operationally. Thus, an organization using the matrix for this purpose may want to know specifically where the data in this domain are defined, produced, and used across the organization.

To go along with adding this information to the Common Data Matrix, the organization may want to record who the data subject matter experts (DSME) and system subject matter experts (SSME) are in the information technology or systems part of the organization. These people can become involved if and when necessary in governance activities pertaining to the data they know.

STEP 2: ASSOCIATE ROLES WITH DATA DOMAINS

List the data domain steward next to the data domain or subdomains down the left side of the Common Data Matrix rather than under organizational unit columns. Placing the data domain steward under one of the organizational columns of the matrix rather than on the left side of the matrix implies that the domain steward is responsible only for data in his or her part of the organization rather than the organization as a whole.

As mentioned earlier, it may be difficult to identify an individual or individuals who have a high level of accountability or decision-making authority for a domain of data across an organization. This is the largest hurdle to overcome when documenting and governing data as a cross-organizational asset rather than as a siloed business unit asset.

A data domain steward may be associated with an entire domain of data or a domain partitioned into subsets. For example, a registrar at a university may be accountable for the entire data domain of *student,* whereas other individuals may have accountability for subsets of that domain. Again, the granularity with which you define domains and the sub-domains may dictate how many data domain stewards you recognize or the subset of the organization's data for which the data domain steward is accountable. Please refer to Chapter 7 for a complete description of the data domain steward.

CASE STUDY: BANK DEFINES A CUSTOMER DATA STEWARD

A large bank in the southeastern United States struggled to identify the person who would have responsibility for the customer data domain across the enterprise. In fact, no one in the organization was knowledgeable about the customer data domain as it pertained to multiple business units. Because of this, the organization struggled to place a person in the role of customer data domain steward. Nobody in the organization could make a decision about customer data for the entire organization without gaining critical feedback from all of the areas of the organization that defined, produced, and used customer data.

Fortunately, the bank didn't force anyone into this critical role. An individual with knowledge of customer data in one part of the organization volunteered to become the data domain steward. He understood that he wouldn't have the responsibility for making decisions that could negatively affect any other part of the organization.

Bank management did, however, volunteer to facilitate discussions across the organization on issues pertaining to cross-organizational use of customer data. This helped to gain consensus on how specific customer data would be defined, produced, and used throughout the bank.

This person was not accountable by himself for making the call when tough decisions couldn't be made. When consensus couldn't be reached, the information regarding the decision was escalated to the data governance council at the strategic level so that the cross-organizational decision could be made.

STEP 3: ORGANIZE COLUMNS

Start with an organizational chart beginning with the top of the organization, break down into business units, and then subgroup into functional areas within the business units, and so on. The information filled in at the top of the Common Data Matrix is typically much easier to define.

Keep in mind that the goal of the Common Data Matrix is to cross reference the data of the organization by subject area with the parts of the organization that define, produce, and use that data and where they define, produce, and use that data.

The Common Data Matrix is also used to record the data governance roles associated with the different parts of an organization. For example, a data governance council member may represent an entire business unit or a subset of that business unit. The alternate person for the council may represent the entire council.

The data steward coordinator may coordinate the activities of the data stewards for a complete business unit or a subset of that business unit. Again, it depends on how granular you define your program and the organizational level of specificity to which you want to govern data.

STEP 4: FILL IN THE CELLS

Store metadata critical to the success of the data governance program in the blocks of the Common Data Matrix where the domains (rows) intersect with the organization (columns). These blocks may be used in multiple ways, and the information stored in them is specific to an organization and how an organization uses this tool.

Some organizations just place an "X" in the block where the rows meet the columns or where the subject area of data in the specific data resource is defined, produced or used in this part of the organization. This is the simplest way to use the Common Data Matrix tool.

Other organizations use the names of individuals who define, produce, and use data in that system in that part of the organization. This becomes a more complex use of the matrix, especially when there are numerous stewards in that part of the organization. Other ways of filling in these blocks include identifying the system of record for that type of data for the organization, how those data flow through the organization, or specifying whether that part of the organization has responsibility for defining those data for the organization, producing those data for the organization, or are just using data in that specific application.

CASE STUDY: GOVERNMENT AGENCY PINPOINTS KEY DATA RESOURCES FOR DIVISIONS

A government agency implementing data governance identified a key resource for each of its divisions. This resource would be represented on its data governance project team to ensure that the interests of each division would be taken into account in the development of the program. The idea for defining the project team this way was that each of these individuals would transition to a program role once the project evolved into a program.

During the development phase of the program, project team members were identified across the Common Data Matrix associated with the divisions they represented. After the project evolved into the program of deploying data governance across the agency, these same individuals played a coordinating role for their divisions for the rollout across the enterprise. Again, their program roles were associated with their parts of the organization rather than with the organization as a whole.

The agency used the Common Data Matrix to record the individuals' names and the parts of the organization they represented for the project and for the program phases.

CASE STUDY: UNIVERSITY CREATES ITS DATA MATRIX

A large university in the southern United States created what it called a University Data Matrix. Data governance supported a directive from the chancellor that data would be classified and handled according to the data sensitivity rules outlined in a new data classification policy. The classifications used were 1) highly confidential data, 2) sensitive data, and 3) public data. Data handing rules were associated with each of the classification levels.

Common data resembled a traffic signal with red used to identify highly confidential data. Yellow identified sensitive data or data that had to be handled according to specific rules defined by the university. Green denoted data that were open and publically available by law.

This university also used the letters of the acronym "CRUD" to define whether that classification of data was created, read, used, or deleted in each of its numerous business areas. The Common Data Matrix documented the specific relationship each part of the university had to the classified data, how classified data needed to be handled, and how the data governance program would operate.

Key Points

- Follow these four steps to complete your Common Data Matrix:

  1. Complete data categorizations by first defining subject areas of data meaningful to your organization.

  2. List the data domain steward next to the data domain or subdomains down the left side of the Common Data Matrix rather than under organizational unit columns.

  3. Start with an organizational chart beginning with the top of the organization, then broken down into business units, then sub-grouped into functional areas of the business units, and so on.

  4. Store metadata critical to the success of the data governance program in the blocks of the Common Data Matrix where the domains (rows) intersect with the organization (columns).

Chapter 12
Data Governance Tools – Activity Matrix

The Governance Activity Matrix is similar to the Common Data Matrix in that it is a two-dimensional matrix that can be customized for use specifically by the organization implementing data governance. Implementing this tool may be completed in many different ways, and like the Common Data Matrix, the cost of developing and using this tool is minimal.

The idea of the governance activity matrix is to cross-reference the steps of a process dealing with data with roles you identify for inclusion in your data governance program. This may sound simple, but you need to consider several things when using this tool.

The first consideration is properly naming the tool and the processes that are governed. The second consideration is what processes will be governed and what it means to govern a process. The third consideration is what information will be collected and used within the tool itself.

AVOID THE TERM "DATA GOVERNANCE PROCESS"

The term "data governance process" contradicts everything about the non-invasive approach to data governance. First and foremost, governance can be applied to any process. Second, just because processes become governed, they don't become data governance processes.

By calling them "data governance processes," we imply that the processes are followed purely because of data governance. But this is typically not the case at all. In fact, you can view almost any process as a form of governance itself, as long as the process is followed.

An ADLC or an SDLC (Application or System Development Lifecycle Methodology) is a form of governance for the development of an application or system. This methodology states the steps to follow in the development, who's involved, the decision that'll be made, the outcome from each step of the methodology, and other things. ADLCs have been around as long as there have been data and systems. Some organizations follow this methodology more closely than others.

The agile development community often appears at odds with the data management community; bringing the two together will be the focus of my next book. But again, the agile approach is, in itself, another type of governance.

The point is, we should not rename the methodology as a "data governance methodology" simply because we appropriately focus on the data according to the steps and involvement throughout the process.

The same holds true for the process of sharing data, the process for requesting access to data, or the process of deleting data. Many organizations have processes for how they do these things. The processes need not to be relabeled as "data governance processes." This label implies that data governance is the reason why we have these processes in place in the first place.

If we want people to know we are non-invasive in our approach to data governance, the last thing we want to do is label processes as governance processes. Rather we explain why we avoid calling them governance processes and that we can either follow these processes formally or consider them for what they are.

PROCESSES TO GOVERN

Organizations determine, in several ways, which processes will be governed or fall under the auspices of data governance. For example, governing the ADLC is one way of building the data focus into every step of new development. Governing data-sharing agreements is another. Governing how we solve data issues may be a third way.

The first question to ask may be, "How do you want to apply data governance at your organization?" Do you want to apply governance proactively by building it into a day-to-day process? Or do you want to build governance into the way you solve issues and address problems? The truth is that most organizations want to do both. In any case, most organizations start reactively by building governance into improving the quality and value of data and slowly building governance into their daily routines.

PROACTIVE DATA GOVERNANCE

The example below demonstrates how an organization built data governance activities into the steps they were following to systematically restructure data in their data warehouse. In this instance, you can see that the activity matrix highlighted the steps of the repeatable process down the left side of the matrix while including the different roles associated with the data governance program across the top.

In each block where the process bisects with the role, you'll see a description of what the person in that role accomplished during that step of the process. In this example, the amount of time that role is expected to play in each step of the process is defined with the period of time that role is expected to be involved.

DG Roles & Level (>) Data Dictionary Valid Process (v)	Estimated effort	Data Governance Team (DGT) *Support Level*	Information Technology (IT) *Support Level*	Data Governance Council *Strategic Level*	Data Domain Stewards *Tactical Level*	Data Stewards *Operational Level*
1. Organize & rationalize 250 reports associated with data warehouse to determine 100 most used & important data element needs.	August– September 2014 (6 weeks) To analyze 250 reports to identify 100 enterprise data elements for data warehouse restructure.	Manage the organization & rationalizing of 250 data warehouse reports. Identify data element usage on the reports to determine 100 most important data element needs. *(16 hours per week per 2 people)*	Supply list and access to technical data warehouse reports. Participate in rationalizing of the reports & identifying of data elements. Record definition of data elements in business glossary. *(8 hours per week per 2 people)*	Approve list of most important data elements. *(1 hour to review and approve data elements)*	Work alongside DGT to rationalize all data warehouse reports to identify most important data elements. *(8 hours per week per Subject Area)*	Supply list & access to data warehouse reports. Participate in rationalizing of the reports & identifying of data elements. Record definition of data elements in business glossary. *(8 hours per week per Business Unit)*
1.1 Define Selection Criteria:						

DG Roles & Level (>) Data Dictionary Valid Process (v)	Estimated effort	Data Governance Team (DGT) *Support Level*	Information Technology (IT) *Support Level*	Data Governance Council *Strategic Level*	Data Domain Stewards *Tactical Level*	Data Stewards *Operational Level*
Reports group, Frequency of use (daily, weekly), data elements used (commonality), criticality, with different results between Business Objects® versions.						
1.2 Define and document: objectives, goals and expected benefits of restructuring the data elements.						
1.3 Define templates and procedures to get the final results.						
1.4 Define the top ten most critical reports (Quick win).						
1.5 Set up success criteria for these reports.						
1.6 Identify the data analyst to contribute to the record definition (producers/users of the reports chosen).						
1.7 Agree and Close the "planning" to finish this "project"						

DG Roles & Level (>) **Data Dictionary Valid Process (v)**	Estimated effort	Data Governance Team (DGT) *Support Level*	Information Technology (IT) *Support Level*	Data Governance Council *Strategic Level*	Data Domain Stewards *Tactical Level*	Data Stewards *Operational Level*
2. Analyze & record definitions in the business glossary. Identify list of data elements that will be included in the data warehouse restructure.	September – October 2014 *(6 weeks)*	Manage the analysis of the data element definitions. Document the data warehouse restructure requirements and the enterprise data element standards. *(16 hours per week per 2 people)*	Provide technical and systems information about the most important data elements. *(8 hours per week per 2 people)*		Provide enterprise business view of most important data elements. Define and document the data element standards in the business glossary. *(8 hours per week per Subject Area)*	Provide business information to include in the definition of the most important data elements. *(8 hours per week per Business Unit)*
2.1 For each report: Identify the results.						
2.2 Identify the data elements that appear.						
2.3 Match the existence of the definition in the data dictionary						
2.4 Validate the definition or gap (by adding a new one…).						
2.5 Close the report data element definitions.						
2.6 Introduce the new definition for approval, then add to data dictionary.						

REACTIVE DATA GOVERNANCE

Many organizations begin their data governance programs by solving known data issues. And they provide a way for people of the organization to record and communicate problems they have with the data they define, produce, and use.

These organizations often standardize the processes they follow to resolve their data issues and to apply governance to these reactive processes.

The example below demonstrates how one organization defined the steps of the process to resolve data issues and to cross-reference the steps someone would need to be involved with using concepts borrowed from the commonly referred RACI assignment matrix. In this way, the organization identified which role was responsible and accountable, who got consulted, and who was informed during the steps of the process.

As mentioned earlier, I've seen organizations add the letter "S" to RACI to change it to RASCI. Including the "S" shows who should support the data governance process.

CASE STUDY: FINANCIAL INSTITUTION PLACES ACTIVITY MATRIX ON ITS INTRANET

A large financial institution took the use of the activity matrix to the next level by incorporating the matrix into the main page on its intranet with its data governance program. After entering the main site, visitors were asked about their level of competency and understanding around subjects related to the governance of their data.

This institution used governance activity matrices as their main proposition around filling in the gaps of knowledge for the organization. The institution provided links to the role descriptions, to the processes that were governed and to in-depth descriptions of how each role was to interact with others associated with the process that was governed.

This organization used the tools to get people involved at the right times in the processes and found the matrix to be helpful in communicating key points around data governance.

Data Issue Resolution Process – Governance Activity Matrix

Data Issue Resolution: regulatory changes, data process improvements, data problems that needs to be corrected, ...

		DATA GOVERNANCE COUNCIL* (STRATEGIC)	DATA GOVERNANCE TEAM* (SUPPORT)	DATA DOMAIN STEWARD (TACTICAL)	DATA STEWARDS (OPERATIONAL)	INFORMATION TECHNOLOGY (SUPPORT)
IDENTIFICATION AND DOCUMENTATION	DATA GOVERNANCE INITIATED EVENT TRIGGERED, DGT MADE AWARE & ENGAGED	I / A	I / R	R	R	S / R
	IDENTIFY DATA AND STAKEHOLDERS ASSOCIATED WITH / IMPACTED BY EVENT USING COMMON DATA MATRIX	I	R	R	I	S
	GATHER EDM AND/OR DATA DOCUMENTATION AND DESCRIBE POTENTIAL SOLUTIONS	*	R	R	I	S
RATIFICATION	ENGAGE STAKE HOLDERS, POINTS OF VIEW HEARD, OPTIONS IDENTIFIED, SOLUTION CHOSEN	A / I	R	C	C	S
	INFORM STAKEHOLDERS OF SELECTED SOLUTION	I	R	I	I	S
IMPLEMENTATION AND CONTROL	IMPLEMENT AND TEST SOLUTION	*	R	C / R	C	S / R
	DOCUMENT AND COMMUNICATE SOLUTION	I	R	C	I	S / R
	MEASURE COMPLIANCE AND COMPLETION OF SOLUTION	I / A	R	C	I	S

R – Responsible for doing the work.
A – Accountable for making certain work is done.
S – Supportive of the work.
C – Consulted on the work.
I – Informed of the work that is done.

Again, there are many ways to use the activity matrix tool and its use becomes the responsibility of the people guiding the data governance program and making certain that data governance is applied consistently across the processes of the organization.

Other examples of processes where you can apply the governance activity matrix include:

- Resolving or researching data quality issues,

- Identifying and monitoring risk and compliance needs,

- Monitoring the data quality lifecycle,

- Validating and gaining approval for data governance metrics,

- Building information vocabulary templates and glossary, and

- Identifying business information needs.

Basically any process where it's important to involve the right people at the right time.

Key Points

- A Data Governance Activity Matrix consists of a two dimensional chart that cross references the data of an organization with data governance activities of each of the roles and responsibilities.

- This matrix enables an organization to quickly see where the impact of changes to data activities will be reflected across the organization.

- The Data Governance Activity Matrix should include business units and specific responsibilities across business units at the top of the matrix, and the data activities, such as data migration tasks, data quality tasks, and master data tasks, already included in project activities along the left side of the matrix.

Many data governance programs focus primarily on communications. Even better, they concentrate on improving communications around managing data and information as a valued enterprise asset. In fact, numerous organizations include communications specialists on their data governance teams who have responsibility for defining, developing, and deploying their data governance programs.

In this vein, the last tool related to data governance is the communications matrix. Like the two other matrices reviewed in Chapters 9 and 10, this is a two-dimensional matrix. Here, you cross reference what you want to communicate with whom you want to communicate it.

For example, you may want to communicate charter and principles, role-based activities of your data governance program—metadata and documentations available, performance metrics, and types of events that will alert or trigger data governance actions.

Before I introduce the communications matrix, it makes sense to talk about a non-invasive approach to how we view communications around data governance. This view includes the distinction of separating the communications that use the tool into three distinct levels. Each of these levels just so happens to start with the letter "O," so I've labeled them as the Three O's of Data Governance Communications: Orientation Communications, Onboarding Communications, and Ongoing Communications.

ORIENTATION COMMUNICATIONS

The first data governance communication level is orientation. This level of communications typically takes place when an individual or group joins the organization or gets promoted to a new position within an organization. Many organizations already provide a level of orientation communications including classroom, or recorded information, about the organization's mission, senior management's vision, facility security information, employee and ID information—basically everything a new hire needs to know to operate effectively within an organization.

Often, orientation sessions include information about data security, privacy, compliance, interacting with social media, and other policies that have become mainstays of the ever-blossoming information age. This information, as well, is focused on educating new hires on how to follow the rules and keep the organization and its reliability and reputation as squeaky clean as possible.

Given the importance of data governance, it may be time to include information about data governance in these orientation sessions. Data governance does not *require* a separate section in these sessions. But then again, maybe that would make sense in your organization, if your organization recognizes the data-as-an-asset philosophy.

It's more likely that data governance could be included as a sidebar to an existing category of information provided. Information about data governance would be a logical extension in any area associated with risk management.

Information about data governance could also be linked to the mission and vision of the organization. Many organizations are calling out the management and use of data and information in their information-age visions.

Is it asking a little too much of an organization to spell out how data governance relates to the mission and vision of an organization? We can always hold out hope, can't we?

A simple list of three items to include in orientation related to data governance would cover:

- The fact that a part of the organization is focused on governing its data. This requires some explanation of what "governance" is, but the explanation can be short.

- The function of data governance in the organization, and...

- Why to, how to, and when to contact somebody in the governance area. Setting up an email address for this works well.

I'm certain we can share other information about data governance with new hires during their orientations. Sometimes, it just takes a creative mind to come up with ways to make people in the organization aware of their role in the governance of data.

A recent client is considering making everybody a deputy data steward, even if all employees don't participate directly in program activities. This organization will give everybody a badge to hang above their desks, if they so choose, that empowers them to have an impact on the quality and use of data within the organization. Damn good idea if people play along! Definitely catchy.

ONBOARDING COMMUNICATIONS

The second data governance communication level is onboarding. Many organizations use this term to describe the activity of getting someone to participate in the data governance program. In other words, onboarding describes what it takes to bring people onboard the data governance ship, if you think of this as such.

This level of communications is obviously important. That's why it's critical for these materials to be well thought out and directly associated with a specific person's involvement in your organization's data governance activities.

Onboarding materials can include the following:

- Data governance charter, guidelines, policy, or whatever works at your organization,

- Data governance best practices and an assessment of present vs. desired state,

- Roles and responsibilities associated with the program,

- Specific, role-based activities associated with a person's role,

- Samples of processes where data governance is being applied,

- Tools and artifacts, e.g. new information, that result from the data governance program, and

- How to use the tools and artifacts to assist them with their jobs.

Some organizations have gone so far as certifying people within their organizations as stewards of the data. I think this makes a lot of sense because the parallels between onboarding and certifying are many.

I don't feel it's appropriate for outside sources to certify data stewards in a public or industry forum. In my opinion, the onboarding process should be specific to the activities of the data governance program within a specific organization.

I'm certain you could include other items in the onboarding process. Basically, consider onboarding as the process to provide individuals and groups with the tool-kit they need to perform their jobs. The tool-kit analogy is perfect here, as it describes what you're providing and how it will be useful to them.

ONGOING COMMUNICATIONS

This brings us to the third level of data governance communication: Ongoing. Ongoing communications include any type of communications that occurs or reoccurs throughout the course of the effectiveness of the data governance program.

It's not effective enough just to orient and onboard people into the program. Ongoing communications often lies at the core of a program that demonstrates success for a substantial period of time. Ongoing communications keeps data governance in everybody's consciousness as they perform their daily activities.

Examples of ongoing communications include:

- Alerts and triggered events of occurrences that require data governance,

- Introduction and changes to the availability of tools and artifacts of data governance,

- Refreshers in the orientation and onboarding materials,

- Performance metrics of the effectiveness of the data governance program,

- Regular minutes and notes from the scheduled data governance council meeting,

- Changes and updates to regulatory and compliance issues, and

- Changes and updates to business rules associated with day-to-day business activities.

Again, I'm certain that other types of communications may need to take place about data governance on an ongoing basis. This is just a starter list.

USING THE COMMUNICATIONS MATRIX

If you look across the top of the matrix on the next page, you'll see that we label the different roles associated with the Operating Model of Roles and Responsibilities spelled out in Chapter 7. The colors between the operating model and the communications matrix are coordinated so that an organization can see the relationship between the role in the model and the types of communications required.

At this point, the question becomes: What goes into each of these blocks? The answer is information that assists in formalizing communications awareness, cross-referencing content, and formally identifying communications roles. In each of these blocks, you'll want to identify who the audience is, the content you're going to provide them, the key message you want to communicate with them, and the media—meeting, website, newsletter, email, etc.—you'll use to deliver information to them, and when you'll communicate information to them.

Communication Plan Matrix

COMMUNICATION TYPES ↓	GROUP 1		GROUP 2	GROUP 3	GROUP 4	
GROUPS → DATA GOVERNANCE ROLES	SENIOR MANAGEMENT STEERING COMMITTEE (EXECUTIVE LEVEL)	DATA GOVERNANCE COUNCIL (STRATEGIC LEVEL)	DATA DOMAIN STEWARDS (TACTICAL LEVEL)	DATA STEWARDS (OPERATIONAL LEVEL)	INFORMATION TECHNOLOGY (SUPPORT LEVEL)	DATA GOVERNANCE PARTNERS (SUPPORT LEVEL)
ORIENTATION COMMUNICATIONS						
PROGRAM PRESENCE & AWARENESS						
ON-BOARDING COMMUNICATIONS						
CHARTER AND PRINCIPLES						
ROLE-BASED ACTIVITIES						
GOVERNANCE DOCUMENTATION						
ON-GOING COMMUNICATIONS						
PERFORMANCE METRICS						
ALERTS & TRIGGERED EVENTS						
COUNCIL / MINUTES / MASS COMM						

The way you communicate with this group differs from the way you communicate to operational data, IT, and everyone else in the organization. All we're doing here is breaking down who needs to be communicated with, and how you're going to communicate with them. All of which we can visualize in this data governance communications matrix:

- **Audience.** Clearly identify your audience. Who needs to hear? Who will be affected? Is the communication for an internal or external organizational unit (district, department, division, section, program, project), role (managers, project managers, stewards), responsibility (through the data management life cycle such as collecting data), or individual (where support from that person is particularly crucial)?

- **Message and Desired Action.** Articulate what you want the audience to learn and what action they need to take. Consider what your audience cares about, such as what's changing, how they are impacted, and what's in it for them, if they support you.

- **Time and Communications Vehicle.** How much time do you have available and what is your method of communication? Is this a 30-second elevator speech? A 3-minute status report at a team meeting? A 30-minute phone call? A 2-hour training session? A face-to-face meeting? A website article? Or a dashboard with metrics?

- **Role within the Data Governance Framework.** What's the audience's role within the data governance framework—executive, strategic, tactical, operational, or support?

Key Points

- There are three types of communications: orientation communications, onboarding communications, and ongoing communications.

- Once the communications plan is developed, the fun of creating all of the material to communicate and the actual communicating of the material begins.

- Above all, it's critical for organizations to recognize that someone has to have the responsibility for following through on the communications plan.

Chapter 14
The End Is Only the Beginning

The time has come for me to put the finishing touches on this Non-Invasive Data Governance book. As I mentioned in the beginning, this book has been a long time coming. The problem was not that I didn't have the materials available to me. The problem was getting the words down on paper so that the content and flow of the book would be beneficial to all of its readers.

When I coined the phrase "Non-Invasive Data Governance" close to ten years ago, it was an expression that described the first approach I took in implementing stewardship for data at a large Blue Cross Blue Shield plan in Pittsburgh in the early 90s. Little did I know that it would become the passion behind my own consulting company, a reason for this book, and a way that I could benefit the organizations implementing data governance and their customers, members, students, participants, and partners in whatever business the organization was in.

As a data administrator for the Blues early in the 90s, I thought I was early to the breed. To learn what it meant to be a data administrator, I subscribed to several technology-based magazines. I came across an article by Larry English titled "Accountability to the Rescue." The article stated that we could improve everything about data—the quality, the protection, compliance, interoperability, and value. This basically came to the rescue with data management, by applying accountability to managing data as an asset. And yes, people in the know did use the term, "data as an asset," even back then.

Several times I've gone back and tried to locate that article on the Internet to no avail. I've lost touch with Larry over the years, but before we lost track of each other, I made certain to thank him for writing that piece and to let him know he helped me set a new direction for my career. Larry and I had several discussions regarding Non-Invasive Data Governance over the years. I owe a lot to Larry. We all owe a lot to him.

Larry used the term "information steward" to describe people who had accountability for data. The Non-Invasive Data Governance approach focuses on helping everybody who defines, produces and uses data in an organization. This is basically everybody, including the operational data stewards, to be held formally accountable for how they define, produce, and use data.

The key word here is "accountability." It's been my belief since my early days in data management that everybody is a data steward. I have stated that managers will be the first to tell you that everybody needs to be held accountable. They will question why people right now are not held formally accountable, and they may go as far as saying that we need to do everything in our power to hold our people accountable. To me, this is common sense.

A great question I often get is, "How do we hold everybody accountable?" And my answer is through the Non-Invasive Data Governance approach. People are already informally accountable. Let's formalize that accountability rather than handing it to people as something that's entirely new.

I'll use this last chapter to remind you of some of the most important aspects of the Non-Invasive Data Governance approach and wrap up the book with the Data Governance "Bill of "Rights."

SUMMARIZING THE NON-INVASIVE DATA GOVERNANCE APPROACH

Non-Invasive Data Governance is communicated as something that already takes place in your organization in an informal, inefficient, and often ineffective manner. The Non-Invasive Data Governance approach focuses on formalizing existing levels of accountability and addressing lapses in formal accountability, and it typically costs only the time put into the effort. In other approaches, data governance is communicated as expensive, complex, time consuming, and over and above the existing work culture of an organization. Remember:

- **Being non-invasive with the approach is less intimidating and threatening**. The Non-Invasive Data Governance approach is designed to fit the culture of an organization and to take advantage of existing levels of governance. It's not an encroachment. In other approaches, data governance is viewed as a discipline that adds unnecessary rigor and bureaucracy to business processes, thus slowing delivery cycles and making data more difficult to access and use.

- **By staying non-invasive with the approach, people see that governance adds value rather than impeding progress**. Expectations about the Non-Invasive Data Governance approach are set by assisting business areas to recognize what they *cannot* do because the data of an organization will not support their activities. With other approaches, data governance expectations are set by the team of individuals responsible for the design and implementation of the data governance program.

- **Mapping data governance to solving business issues helps to describe data governance as something a business needs rather then what "data people" want to put in place**. With non-invasive data governance, individuals are identified and recognized with roles associated with their existing relationship to data—as data definers, producers, users, subject-matter experts, and decision makers. With other approaches, individuals are assigned new roles as part of their involvement in a data governance program.

- **Recognizing people for their relationships to data and helping them to understand that how they manage data impacts people and businesses across an enterprise**. With non-invasive data governance, individuals' job titles do not change, and it is acknowledged that the vast majority of their responsibilities will not change. With other approaches, individuals are given the title of "Data Steward," and their job responsibilities are adjusted accordingly.

- **The people of your organization have day jobs.** Unless you change their "day jobs" (very difficult to do), people will have to absorb their steward responsibilities for data governance to succeed. In the Non-Invasive Data Governance approach, more than one data steward—a formally accountable person—is associated with each type of data. That's because an organization recognizes that multiple people share this association with data, i.e. multiple users of particular data. With other approaches, individuals are assigned as individual data stewards for specific subject areas of data.

- **Everybody stewards data depending on their relationship to data**. Organizations apply non-invasive data governance principles to existing work flows and processes by formalizing discipline, accountability, and involvement around these processes. With other approaches, organizations refer to processes as "data governance processes." Doing so incorrectly gives the impression that the processes are carried out, because of the data governance program.

- **Data governance is all about the execution of authority over the management of data and data-related assets**. The authority comes through the application of governance to existing processes and workflows. In other words, getting the "right" people involved in the "right" process … Read the next section for the complete Data Bill of "Rights." The truth is that a Non-Invasive Data Governance program can be managed from a business unit or information technology (IT) unit, as the business areas and ITs hold specific knowledge and formal accountability relative to governing data as a valued enterprise effort.

DATA GOVERNANCE BILL OF RIGHTS

As Wikipedia tells us, "A bill of rights is a list of the most important rights to the citizens of a country. The purpose of these bills of rights is to protect these rights against infringement."

The term "bill of rights" originated in England. Here, the term refers to the Bill of Rights enacted by Parliament in 1689, following the Glorious Revolution, asserting the supremacy of Parliament over the monarch and listing a number of fundamental rights and liberties.

You may ask yourself what this has to do with data and data governance. My answer is: everything and nothing. I could have written about the rights of employees or members of your organization to have high quality data that better enables them to perform in their job functions. I'd hasten to add that it's the goal of any data governance program to provide these individuals with data and information that helps them and their organizations succeed.

Instead, I've chosen to summarize this book by writing about specifically different rights of a data governance program. By this, I mean the right things to do to get your data governance program to operate the way you want it to. This Data Governance Bill of Rights consists of the right behaviors needed and expected to achieve the optimum results from your data governance program.

My definition of data governance is: **The execution and enforcement of authority over the management of data and data related assets.**

And my definition of data stewardship is: **The formalization of accountability over the management of data and data-related assets.**

This is about the enforcement of authority through the formalization of accountability that best describes a Non-Invasive Data Governance program. Taken together, the enforcement and formalization require:

- Getting the **Right** People,

- Involved at the **Right** Time,

- In the **Right** Way,

- Using the **Right** Data,

- To make the **Right** Decision, and

- Leading to the **Right** solution.

Let's review these points one by one.

GETTING THE RIGHT PEOPLE

This is perhaps the easiest right to address. These individuals define, produce, and use your data. You inventory the data—not necessarily all your data—and cross reference your data with these individuals or parts of the organization that define, produce and use the data.

This may sound like a monstrous task, but the truth is it can, and should, be done incrementally. You can complete this just by using information about who was involved during recent and present data-focused initiatives. The best tool to conduct this inventory is the Common Data Matrix discussed in Chapter 11.

INVOLVED AT THE RIGHT TIME

To address this right, simply use the Data Governance Activity Matrix, also presented in Chapter 12. A caveat here: Just because you create a Data Governance Activity Matrix for a specific process or procedure doesn't turn this process or procedure into something called a data governance process. If you call something a data governance process, you define data governance as the villain and as an additional burden on individuals that slows things down. The fact is all processes can be governed, whether or not data governance is involved.

IN THE RIGHT WAY

This may be the most difficult right to get right. This right involves making certain that the steps down the left side of the Data Governance Activity Matrix are the correct or at least, most appropriate actions to take.

This is where data governance really comes to life, or becomes difficult depending on your perspective. Completing a Data Governance Activity Matrix for your system development life cycle (SDLC) can be simple because the steps of the process already exist and can be leveraged.

Completing a Data Governance Activity Matrix to make sure regulatory and compliance rules are captured, communicated, and followed can be complex.

This right is the most critical of the Data Bill of "Rights." The methodologies, processes, and best practices most likely exist somewhere in your organization. If you simply cross reference the properly governed steps of the activity with the right people, you're taking steps to formalize accountability and to become more efficient and effective in your processes and most likely in the governance of data.

USING THE RIGHT DATA

This right can be tricky as well. Many organizations have no definition of what right data is. This makes it all the more difficult to fix the wrong data or get to the right answers.

For example, let's say you have an enterprise-data warehouse that's working perfectly and you have a master data solution in place; you know where your systems of record are for your data and can direct people to these data. If all this is true, your situation is pretty good.

If you've governed the steps of your formalized process (see previous rights), you can apply pointing to the right data as part of your processes. Does this make sense? My recommendation is to make getting to the right data an important part of the processes and procedures you govern.

TO MAKE THE RIGHT DECISION

Often, the right decision is based on the right data, but not always. Getting the right decision is often based on the right person making that decision with the right data.

Ultimately, right data leads to the right decision. But often no assurance exists that a decision is correct until time has passed, and you validate the decision through business activity.

At the risk of sounding obvious, let me say that for the right decision to work out right, the solution that follows this decision must also be right. This may fall back on the use of a Data Governance Activity Matrix to map the steps used to follow through on the right decision.

LEADING TO THE RIGHT SOLUTION

Now, we come to the end of the Data Governance Bill of Rights and this book. Getting to the right solution is the purpose of your data governance program. I can't think of a simpler way to describe what your data governance program should do.

If you approach your senior managers and tell them you have an easy way to get the right people involved at the right time in the right way using the right data to get to the right decisions and solutions, they'll most likely ask you how. This is where you fall back and use the tools mentioned in Chapters 9, 10 and 11.

I hope you've found this book to be helpful. Please feel free to contact me to discuss how the Non-Invasive Data Governance approach works for you and your organization: rseiner@kikconsulting.com.

Good luck to you and your team. And remember:

Get started and stay non-invasive.

Index

Bold page numbers indicate definitions

Printed in Great Britain
by Amazon